The Necessary Goat
and other essays

Contents

Foreword

To give passion a legitimate outlet and to show the direction in which it should flow, like a river, for the benefit of a whole country, is the common problem of mankind.

I. Goncharov
Oblomov

It was during a two-year period as Fellow in Creative Writing at Jordanhill College, Glasgow, that I became interested in the nature of creativity. It did not happen through any dispassionate curiosity; quite the reverse. It sprang from a powerful emotional discomfort, the causes of which were obscure though clearly connected in some way with the work I was doing. This work was a departure from my normal occupation as a writer, and it gave me a taste of the relatively uncreative life which is nowadays regarded as normal, and raised the first suspicions that it is not, in fact, normal at all.

I make no apology for detailing the effects of this imposed uncreativity, for many thousands of people suffer some degree of the same distress, accepting it as an inevitable part of living. It has become clear to me that the source of this discomfort is the blocking of a creative mental function which is inherent in all of us, and which is deeply necessary for our well-being. This book attempts to suggest ways in which it can be realised and enhanced.

Alison Prince
Isle of Arran
1990

First Notes

I began my two years at the College with enthusiasm, expecting a wide involvement in the problems of self-expression both in students' own work and in their approach to pupils.

Disappointment set in almost at once. The rigid, tightly-packed timetable left no uncommitted periods, and Creative Writing had no discernible place in preparing young people to be teachers. A few students sought help with their poetry and in one case with a proposed novel, and I put in an occasional "guest appearance" in other tutors' seminars, but the only opportunities which seemed to be of substantial value were several in-service sessions with mature teachers who were doing a degree in their spare time. Increasingly, I accepted invitations to get involved in school-based projects initiated by people who had only a tenuous link with the College.

This was no disadvantage. It gave me a wide experience of Scottish schools and an insight into their problems which is not always granted to the more formal visitor. Wherever I went, I met teachers and librarians who were anxious to encourage creativity among children, particularly in the Primary schools; and yet, often in these very people, there was a confessed lack of self-confidence about the expression of individual feeling. Before an adult in-service session started, there would be defences offered. "I hope you're not expecting me to write." And there would be excuses. "I'm so used to writing reports and factual stuff, I've forgotten how to use my imagination." Most universally of all - "You won't read it out, will you?"

Such need for self-protection speaks of damage done to sensitive, intelligent people during their formative years. Had we been meeting to discuss the drawing-up of a new timetable, nobody would have protested an inability to think in logical and mathematical terms - and this despite a frequently-admitted dislike of mathematics as a subject. A timetable demands no statement of feelings, so it is safe territory, but to write from one's own viewpoint seems alarming. There are no secure rules for doing such a thing, and no clear way of measuring success or failure. The whole area is a minefield of potential embarrassment and vulnerability.

Interestingly, an invitation to write down memories of early childhood is less threatening. A cushioning of time lies between the child who lived then and the adult who lives now, and the memory of the strong feelings which were experienced is sanctioned by the excuse that one was not expected to be clever and sensible. People are often startled by the power and vitality of what they write down. One head teacher said at the end of a session, "I've spent all my life addressing external questions - after this, I feel I should start addressing the internal ones."

Children show a great curiosity about someone who lives by the use of creative ability. They want to see how it connects with something they sense to be part of themselves. Their questions are always the same:

"Did you like writing when you were at school?"
"Why did you want to be a writer?"
"Do you enjoy it?"
"Where do you get your ideas from?"

Teachers ask questions connected with procedure:

"Do you find it hard to be self-disciplined?"
"Do you have a structured work-pattern?"

They nod approvingly as I say that the work is demanding and that I stick at it for long hours, and glance at the children to reinforce the point that there is no escape from effort and regularity. I search fruitlessly for a way to emphasise that procedures cannot initiate ideas, and launch into my theme of living itself being the source of what to write about. The nods become less certain.

These sessions in schools serve to highlight the difficulty of talking about the thought-processes which take place before the products are made manifest. There is no great problem when talking to children of Primary school age, because the understanding of the direct, uncluttered experiencing of life is still there as a common ground between us, but in Secondary schools it begins to crumble. Adults, except in private, talk almost exclusively in terms of structure and procedures.

Creativity, by definition, spans the change of state from having no formal existence to the positive having of such existence. The latter state has a wealth of language to describe it, as the criticism columns in magazines and newspapers make plain, but the former has none. For this reason, creativity is thought of as mysterious, as if it performed the magic trick of making something from nothing.

This is, of course, impossible. Something always comes from something, and creativity is the using of a rich compost of feelings and experience. Unfortunately, the language of feeling is currently considered to be lacking in academic respectability because it attempts to state no finite fact, and so our networks of understanding are limited to what is seen as demonstrable and true. This difficulty of defining what is indefinable became one of the major factors in the mental discomfort which I began to experience at this time. After twenty years of working on my own as a writer, I had become a performer who talks about writing instead of doing it, and the talk could not quite explain what the process was like.

The discomfort took a form which was familiar to me from my own school-days. Institutional buildings with their smells of food and people and residual wet mackintoshes filled me with irrational fury, as did their raucous sounds and the treeless monotony of their prison-yard playgrounds. In the privacy of my own mind, the stream of comment took on a profanity which found an echo of absolute recognition when I read James Kelman's "A Disaffection".

Obviously this protest had something to do with the imposition of a different kind of work-pattern on my normal mental functioning, and I supposed initially that it was a stifling of awareness. In the irritation of being surrounded by people whose concerns were almost exclusively methodological, a narrowing seemed to be affecting my ability to think. I embarked on a deliberate exploration of the depression and fury which had become such an obstruction, trying to suspend all judgment and be open to the truth of experience. It was easier to do this in the natural surroundings of the island where I live than in the city. During this period of investigation, I began to notice things with peculiar clarity. I noted them down as precisely as possible, working them over and over again to delete anything less than central to the experience I was recording. There was some satisfaction in this work, but I could make no progress in analytical terms, except to become more certain that some essential function was being disrupted by the imposition of a life-pattern not of my own designing.

In the second year of the Fellowship I shared the post with another writer, thus halving the time I spent in the College. To my great interest, my job-share colleague began to suffer the same symptoms of fury and impatience within a very short time. This increased my growing conviction that the creative process was a necessary function, strong in those who had developed it but present as a real and integral part of every human mind.

At this stage, thinking in words had become overtaken by this problem about the nature of creativity which seemed to hold the key to the whole puzzle of the situation. Any hope of writing fiction was swamped by this concern, together with its continuing effects. Returning after many years to the discipline in which I had originally trained, I began to draw and paint in a further exploration of awareness.

During this second year my days at the College were more intensively used, and so the conflict between personal awareness and procedural activity also intensified. Sitting over a cup of coffee in Princes Square, the impact of where I was became almost unbearably sharp. I wrote down what was happening.

In the city
Where is there to weep?
The orange trees
Tubbed on the cafe terrace
Mark a boundary,
That's all.
They have not brought
Their grove,
Their fruitfulness,
Their quiet sky, so blue
Between the pointed leaves.
There is no quietness.
A roaring murmur fills the pillared space
With voices, clinking spoons,
Hard heels. An infant cries,
A telephone
Ring-rings,
Ring-rings.

Something is happening
To make my throat contract,
My heart thump suddenly;
A pain, not in the limbs,
But wanting the sea's clean line
Below the quiet sky.
A city pain
Possesses me.
And where is there to weep?

It was obvious that I had reached the end of this particular line of investigation. I felt shaky and beaten, and badly wanted to go home to the natural rhythms of the burn and the trees and the sky, but a few days of the term remained. I went to a Primary school where a teacher was trying particularly hard to encourage the children in creative writing. One little girl was bursting with ideas and intelligent responses, and I commented after the session that this child showed outstanding promise. The teacher shook her head. "She won't do well", she said. "She's inattentive and she doesn't have a good memory, and there's no back-up from home. I'd say she won't go anywhere."

Outrage welled up, but the teacher's practicality could not be denied. What she said was true. At home, I thought about the child as I walked through the forest in the glen, and all the elements began to come together as they had done in the paintings, where I had incorporated human figures into a single entity with rocks and water and the sky. The child was of the natural functioning of life. My assumptions underwent a shift.

As a post-graduate Education student many years ago, I had read

Adlerian psychology, and had accepted the prevailing view that the non-rational part of the mind was a kind of swamp, a formless and mysterious depth from which coherent thoughts occasionally emerged. Now, I perceived this to be a misleading picture. The underlying processes of the mind, far from being inchoate, constitute a precise and delicate machine which is central to our whole being. They supply the material without which top-mind reasoning could not function.

Without yet formulating a clear picture of how this machine could be visualised, I could see what had been wrong with my previous efforts to understand the stress of the situation. The impulse to concentrate on awareness had been caused, not by a reduced ability to feel, as it had seemed at the time, but by a reduced freedom to make use of that ability. I saw that awareness is a continual through-put, just as blood circulates continually through the body. To check the continuum is to apply a partial tourniquet.

We are not static, but in a state of perpetual movement which consists of the ongoing interpretation of experience. This function can happen at a very low "tick-over" level, or at full power, but in any living organism, it cannot stop. Life itself, in these terms, is a creative process.

Visualisation

During the months of difficulty in forming a picture of the creative process, the most stable element in the conundrum was the tall beech tree which grows by the burn not far from my house. Habitually, I begin each morning with a walk, regardless of weather, during which the material for the day's work clarifies itself, and at this time the beech tree began to represent a complete embodiment of the life-process. There was an intake of sustenance from the roots which reached down to the water, followed by the making of thousands of beech-mast children and the continuing growth of the parent body. The water left the tree through the capillaries of twigs and leaves which meshed with the air. Death had already marked it, for the tree's silver-grey trunk was scarred by the tearing away of a limb during a storm.

At one time, the tree was a powerful religious symbol. As "ashera", it represented the female spirit of life, and even in places where no trees grew, a wooden pole would serve the same symbolic purpose. By now, I was beginning to see that life and creativity cannot be separated, but I also began to understand that awareness is equally universal. In the first year of my close attentiveness to the beech tree, there was a warm early spring and the tree unfurled its buds in the first weeks of April, only to have them blasted by May frost. As a result, its leaves were brown-tipped for the rest of the year. In the following spring, there was again an early warm spell, but this time the tree kept its buds tightly furled and did not unroll them until mid-May.

The tree obviously had awareness. In the same way, a dandelion is able to sense its surrounding conditions (or perhaps even to learn from experience), growing tall among long grass but short and stubby on a trodden path. Gardeners have always known this, referring to plants as "greedy" or "shade-loving" or "resentful of transplanting". To recognise this awareness is often confused with attributing human qualities to the plant, but such easy anthropomorphism is no more than a sentimental extension of the self. A plant has a degree of awareness which is directly related to its maximum possible achievement, and so has a human being, but the potential is of a very different order. The similarity is in the mechanics of the process.

This can be seen, in the case of the beech tree, as a very slow fountain, taking in water from the roots and carrying it upward through the living

13

system where it is converted into energy and new tissue. At the ends of the branches, seeds are sent out and surplus water is voided into the air. Diagrammatically, this movement of water looks roughly semicircular.

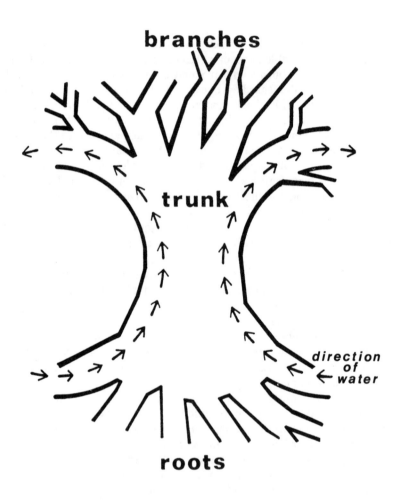

Illustration 1

Obviously, these semicircles cannot exist in a vacuum, for a rotary movement must complete itself, or it has to retract the movement in order to begin it again. In the case of the tree, the nature of this completion is well known, for the water vapour which it puts out into the atmosphere will condense and fall as rain, to be picked up by the roots and begin the cycle again.

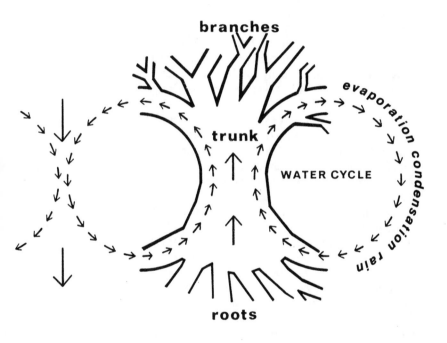

Illustration 2

15

Such circles of movement can be seen in an infinite range of contexts, and the way in which their edges interact in a downward direction is just as interesting and thought-provoking as their more obvious upward interaction within the notional tree. Here, they work almost as cog wheels do, meshing within the substance of the tree to supply it with power.

Whereas water is the essential stuff of a tree's living cycle, together with the nutrients it carries, for the human mind, the basic material of its throughput is experience. This may be as simple as a baby's first awareness of discomfort, or as complex as the reading of a thesis, but without the flow of experience through the mind, there can be no thinking, because there is no awareness of anything to be thought about.

It began to be clear that the process of creativity could be visualised as something akin to a plant's use of water. Growth and development, for the plant, depend on the way in which it stores water and deploys it for its needs, and the same thing is true of humans in their use of experience. We store this raw material as memory and as energy-potential. Children have hardly any reserve stores because they have not had time to accumulate much experience, but the very old are so filled with memories that they lose interest in current experience and are content instead to browse through their richly-stocked store-house. Sometimes, with the stiffness of old age, it is only a few memories which circulate again and again.

If we have to add constantly to our store of experience, then any conceivable model of how this is done must incorporate flexibility. There cannot be emptiness within us, for in some sense the organism which represents creativity is a physical one, and must obey the laws of pressure. A vacuum is not tolerable, so the size of the functioning body must be capable of variation. We are surrounded on all sides by simple living things which have this capacity, so there is no need to try and invent something complex. The easiest and most right-seeming model is a flower bulb. This is an organism which can store all the potential it needs for the dramatic production of blossoms, and when that creative effort is complete, it is left smaller, ready for further storage and re-growth.

Experience, however, is a far more complex raw material than water, and my concern is to determine the way in which it is used in the creative process. Clearly, it arrives in the form of recognisable phenomena, but what happens next? One becomes aware of them, but they must become part of the self before they can be used as material for the making of opinions or actions. We speak or write, not about things, but about the way things make us feel. In some circumstances, it is very difficult to get rid of this feeling-process and arrive at what we hope is an objective statement of the truth. History and science struggle to do this, but without real success. We can only state what seems to be true, and "seeming" is the largest part of the creative intelligence, for it is produced by the flexible and mysterious area of feeling.

16

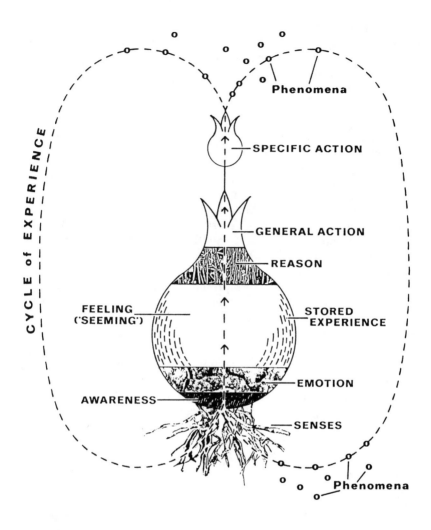

Phenomena

SPECIFIC ACTION

GENERAL ACTION

REASON

FEELING ('SEEMING')

STORED EXPERIENCE

EMOTION

AWARENESS

SENSES

Phenomena

Illustration 3

In this diagram, the bulb represents the self. Its outer skin is the point at which one's own being ends and the external world begins, and it should have the same flexibility as the physical skin, able to stretch and contract according to the state of the contained body.

The "roots" of the self are the senses. They are the means by which we see and hear, feel and smell what is going on around us, so they act to bring experience into the system, just as a bulb's roots bring in water. They act purely mechanically, for they themselves are not aware. They feed their collected phenomena into awareness, which is shown as the dark area at the base of the bulb.

17

A phenomenon, in this context, must be thought of as an experience-package. It may be a simple sensation, such as the warmth of the sun on the skin, or a complex experience such as listening to a Bach chorale or attending a committee meeting, but it arrives as raw material, quite neutrally. Some phenomena are self-produced. To read one's own draft pages written on the previous day is to take in a real experience, as is the resuming of work on a design or painting, or the continuing of a teaching project. Creative work is a self-feeding cycle, which is why it is so satisfactory, but also so demanding.

Awareness has a very simple function, akin to that of the amoeba which registers irritability when touched. It passes the received phenomena through into the system while establishing them as present in the consciousness - but the first layer of the self with which it is in direct contact is emotion. So, when an experience-package arrives, it is brought into the being and passed directly into the emotion-function, where it is invested with the energy of whatever reaction its presence causes. This emotional reaction has no form in itself - it is no more than a force. If, for instance, the senses report the presence of an aggressive, shouting person, the awareness ingests this and passes it through to be clad with fear and anger by the emotions. It is almost as if an incoming sperm must be united with an egg of the body's own production before it can develop into a creative action. In the case of the aggressive person, once fertilised by emotion, it becomes an internalised threat. We have, so to speak, a blastocyst consisting of the external phenomenon plus the self's response to it. "Threat" is in itself an emotional term. It cannot be applied to the original shouting person, because there is no threat until someone feels threatened.

The next stage of the process is shown as the biggest, but it is also the most flexible, being at the broadest part of the bulb where shape can most easily change. This is the "feeling" area, which is large in some people and almost non-existent in others. It is of enormous importance in creativity and in the wise conduct of life generally, but it is little-understood and frequently confused with emotion. The difference between the two is vital. Emotion, coupled with the phenomena to which it is linked, acts as raw fuel, as petrol is to an engine, but feeling is the engine itself.

To make this clear, we can return to the shouting, aggressive person. The effect of this manifestation on the emotions is to produce fear and annoyance, but these reactions in themselves have no substance until they are expressed. Feeling investigates them and develops them into a variety of potential responses, and the scope of these can be very wide in a person whose capacity for feeling-intelligence is broad and well-developed. In someone of narrower capacity, there may be only one or two - in this case, to shout back or to run away. A broadly functioning person may have a moment's dizzying indecision while the possibilities of response are juggled. Smile, ask what's the matter, pretend not to notice, create a diversion (what sort?), scream, faint, run, ignore it....the permutations are endless.

These possibilities exist as potential, but they are not consciously explored until the most insistent of them have come through into the reasoning process, where they are given a direction and stripped of ambivalence. This is shown on the diagram as a vertically-striped area. Within this, a final choice is made as to which alternative will be selected for putting into action, and this choice is passed on into the area of general action, represented as the sprouting leaves at the top of the bulb.

General action implies the normal capacity for moving and thinking and talking which we take for granted, but from this can blossom any number of specific actions, which are completed responses to the incoming experience. In the case of something very urgent and simple such as the touching of a hot oven, the awareness will flash its pain-message at lightning speed through emotion, where it acquires shock-urgency, and through feeling which instantly identifies a need to remove the hand from the hot stove. Reason ratifies it (though it may also pick up a fleeting caution not to drop the dish which is being held) and general action blossoms into the specific activity of taking the hand away.

Such an action happens virtually instantaneously, and there is no lasting result which stays as a permanent thing for other people to experience in their turn as a phenomenon. A much more complex and long-lasting response to experience can, however, be a thing which exists in its own right, and this is where we recognise that a creative act has taken place.

If an artist becomes acutely aware through his or her visual sense that the appearance of something is particularly intriguing, then the awareness will set up emotions of desire and perhaps of ferocity or love which produce a great range of potential interpretation in the feeling-intelligence. From this potential, the reasoning process may select several possibilities, but they can only be put into action one at a time, so a whole series of sketches may result, perhaps followed by a more thoroughly worked-out painting. All these specific actions are given a tangible presence of their own. They can go on existing even after the artist has died, for they are phenomena in their own right, ready to circulate as experience through the creative systems of other people.

To read a book or listen to music or look at a painting is to experience a phenomenon of someone else's making, and this is easy to associate with creativity. We must understand, though, that the blossoming of such self-sufficient constructions as books or musical compositions or pictures can only happen when the underlying process is in a particularly well-developed and healthy state. If we want to encourage creativity, then we must be aware that the process exists in everyone, functioning at a sub-blossoming level which needs food and nurture before it can come to maturity.

Just as flower bulbs start as small things which must develop and grow, so does human creativity, The "roots" of the senses must be given ample space and a rich ground in which to find a ready supply of phenomena, and the awareness must be allowed to grow, feeding the all-important area of feeling-intelligence with emotionally-charged experience. This is where we have in recent years been making an enormous mistake which has resulted in the suppression of creativity; we have denied the importance of feeling.

Increasingly over the last century, we have been encouraged to see feeling as frivolous, self-indulgent and untrustworthy. We regard it as a partisan declaration of opinion which is of no value because it does not seek to provide a neutral common ground. It is no more than a statement of the way things seems to be to a particular observer. We could take a number of such expressions of evidence and use them as co-ordinates to build a conjectural structure, but we do not. Instead, we put our faith in reason, precisely because it seeks to isolate a single fact from all other potentialities and establish it as being objectively true.

This is a life-fearing attitude which speaks of a deep distrust of the human condition. There are religious and historical reasons for it which will be discussed at a later stage, but the major reason for our lack of trust in feeling is that we have never been able to disentangle it from emotion. Consequently, we try to diminish the feeling area and increase the capacity of reason, with results which turn out to be a self-fulfilling prophecy. If we look at a diagram showing a reduced feeling-function, it can be seen at once that emotion is pressed perilously close to reason, and is therefore dangerous. When raw emotion is not digested into a range of potential actions, it barges straight through into the rationalising process, offering no alternative but its own urgency. Hence we get narrow but powerful convictions expressed, often backed by fury or petulance when the holder's views are disagreed with. Such internal imbalance can give rise to fanaticism. (Illustration 4 next page)

Feeling is the essential buffer-state between emotion and reason. Because it is sub-rational and seems to produce things of its own accord, we find it hard to recognise that it is a very real part of our thinking-process and so we tend to discount it, but it can be deliberately used and cultivated.

Much of our difficulty in distinguishing between emotion and feeling is due to our inherited linguistic paucity of description of the two functions (which in turn is due to our historic lack of perception.) The English language, in common with most, contains only the single word, "feel" with which to express three separate things; tactile sensation, emotion, and an effort to perceive the truth.

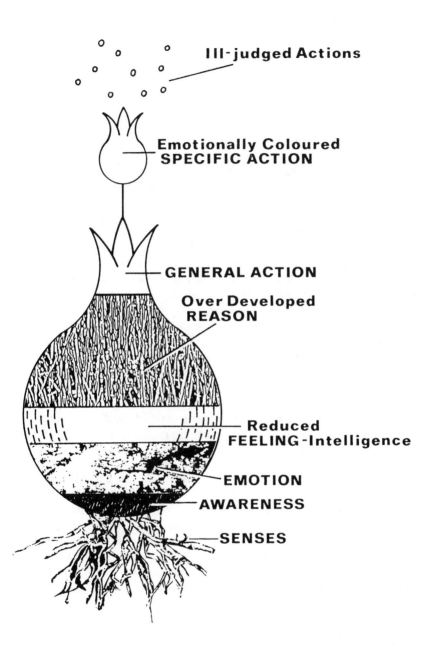

Illustration 4

21

I feel cold
I feel that the cat's fur is soft.

I feel sad.
I feel excited.

I feel that he is not honest.
I feel that our marketing strategy is wrong.
I feel that God is universal intelligence.

The first two statements are about physical sensation, the second two about the state of the emotions, and the last group contains gropings towards perception.

Many people, when considering the last three statements, will have an impulse to substitute the word "think" for the word "feel". This is because, in our current intellectual climate, it is considered more respectable to rely on rational thought-processes than intuitive ones. Feeling is associated with softness and femininity whereas thinking is considered to be a sterner process, free of emotional colouring. And yet, ironically, the very heart of the economic process which underlies all business, the "market" which supplies the rationale of the Western world, is always described in terms of feeling. Bidding is nervous or confident, aggressive or panicky. The delicate balance between currencies and between the values of the various businesses is as temperamental as a prima donna, trembling like some over-bred pedigree animal which may drop dead before it wins the millions its owners and backers hope for. When put to the ultimate test, rationality can only look to the springs of feeling which nourish it. Having brought all known factors into consideration, the outcome still depends on human interpretation. The shrewd dealer is said to "have his finger on the pulse" or even, shruggingly, to be "lucky". Either way, it is an admission that a sense of how the unpredictable market forces will move cannot be acquired by logic alone. The subconscious intelligence of feeling is at work, supplying likelihoods through the process we know as intuition.

In business just as in the arts and sciences, creativity is an essential quality. It may well be, in fact, that our apparent lack of creative people is not because the quality does not exist, but because it is diverted into the service of money-making activities as such. Clearly, this is an idea much favoured by the current government, with its talk of the "enterprise culture". The mistake is to assume that creativity is an accidental attribute rather than a fundamental process. This misunderstanding leads to a very common crisis in the lives of business people, particularly those who have built up a business of their own from small beginnings. At first, the construction of the enterprise is fascinating. It is based on a good idea or a skill, and it grows like a living thing, supplying its creator with a rich feed-back as it develops. At a certain critical stage, however, it becomes too big for its originator to manage alone. Its growth must either stabilise at this point or other people must be brought in to share the work of running it. Either way, it has become established as a continuum; it is no longer essentially the dependent "brain-child" of its maker, and he or she feels a sense of loss. Often this is suppressed and the financial success of the business becomes a substitute for the interest of setting it up. Frequently, the originator will sell it and turn to something else.

The reason for this loss of interest and for the cynicism and world-weariness which follow it is simply that the creative functioning of the originator is no longer actively needed and so it suffers from a deprivation of outlet. It is no accident that company directors play golf or take up painting or dabble in charity work. They are subconsciously seeking for a way to use the frustrated creativity which rages round within them.

People who are actively involved in some means of expression throughout their lives do not arrive at this crisis of boredom and disillusion, for they have a continuingly active creative cycle. Artists and actors, writers, painters and musicians tend to work until the end of their lives, limited only by physical ability. Because they do not hand over their creative functioning for the use of some external structure which results only in the making of money, they never suffer the sense of loss experienced so commonly by business people. They do not suspect uneasily that their popularity is due to their wealth, or wonder why everything seems stale and unrewarding. They have worries, certainly, and panic from time to time when tiredness makes the cycle slow down and it seems as if a death of the soul is setting in - but the fundamental interest in the process of living is always present and endlessly intriguing.

Perhaps in a recognition of this fact, artistic people are regarded these days as being in some way exceptional. Such words as "inspiration" and "talent" are bandied about, emphasising the supposed difference between these and "ordinary" people. This is an entirely artificial division. The flowering of creativity takes place in small acts all the time; in a question asked at a public meeting or the writing of a letter to a friend or even in such trivial-seeming matters as complaining about a dirty glass in a pub. The confidence to do these things comes from an understanding that one is no less and no more than a user of experience, like everyone else.

The habit of creativity is a reliance on one's own capacity to relish experience and, in time, to use it. In non-urgent matters, the cycle works slowly, and much of the experience we encounter is tucked away within the feeling-intelligence as memory. Even if it is not positively used as the raw material for some later product, it serves a vital purpose in the mind, for it provides a reference against which later experiences can be measured. This is why the opinion of an "experienced" person is sought when a puzzling situation is encountered; such a person is equipped with previously-laid-down stores of ingested phenomena against which the latest one can be matched or contrasted. There can be no measuring without a yard-stick, and received opinion cannot supply such a thing, for it is the product of someone else's yard-stick. To build up one's own scale of evaluation demands direct, first-hand experience of all kinds.

As our capacity for economic and technological power has grown, so our respect for non-theoretical experience has dwindled; with it, inescapably, creativity has been suppressed. Full-time compulsory education has only been with us for the last hundred years or so, but it has acted to replace the immediate "how-it-seems" quality of life with a different concept. The subliminal message of the school is clear to the child. Never mind how it seems - you are here to be taught how it ought to be, and how you ought to fit within it. A structure, unsuspected by the young child, begins to be evident. Its verticals and horizontals criss-cross his or her awareness with requirements and prohibitions. Wordsworth called them the "shades of the prison-house". They are only shades, and yet, for thousands of people, they become bars from which there is no escape.

I hold that self-knowledge must come before all things. When one has stripped off all the conventions, and superstitions, and hypocrisies, then one is educated.

A.S. Neill.

Groupings.

If we think again about the 'bulb' diagram of creative functioning, but this time imagine it crowded on either side by other bulbs, it can be seen that the senses of each one will overlap with those of its neighbours. The space in which to develop a broad, freely-cycling feeling-function is restricted by the proximity of others. The cycle of creative work is disrupted because there is no room for the free circulation of experience, just as over-crowded plants do not get the light and moisture which they need. The phenomena which filter through to the senses have a second-hand quality about them, as they have already circulated through the surrounding bodies, much as air in a crowded place circulates through the lungs of all the people present.

In practical terms, this implies that closely-grouped people tend to receive opinion rather than impressions, just as they will see human-made things rather than natural ones. Roads, shop windows, advertisments, buildings, goods for sale, mechanically reproduced music - all these are phenomena produced by humans, often in order to have a specific effect on the receiver.

When daffodil bulbs are over-crowded, their growing tips (equivalent to reason in the creative analogy) continue to produce the general activity of leaves, but their flowering is severely limited by the narrowing of the vital "feeling" area in which the preparation for a specific creative function takes place.

The term "narrow-minded" is surprisingly accurate. It conjures up a person of fixed opinion, unwilling or unable to accommodate any new input of ideas. Such a person will usually have a job which is carried out with meticulous attention to its details, even though these may involve ludicrous departures from common sense. He or she will not be without emotion - far from it. If we look at a diagram of a severely narrowed creative functioning, the reason will become obvious.

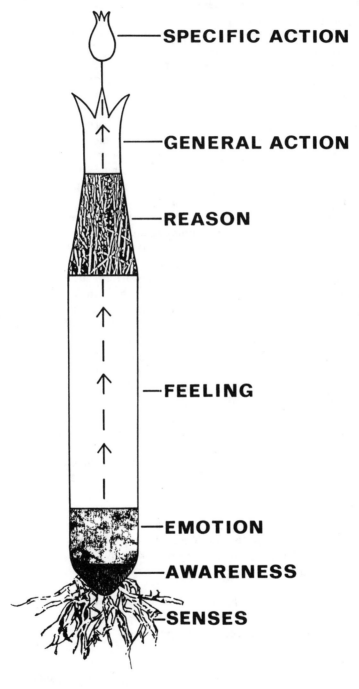

SPECIFIC ACTION

GENERAL ACTION

REASON

FEELING

EMOTION

AWARENESS

SENSES

Illustration 5

Here is a personality shaped and acting rather like a rocket. The proportion of feeling-intelligence is very low compared with the area of reasoning, and so there is no space for the slow, many-channelled explorations of possibility which feeling can provide. Instead, there can only be a straight-line implementation of what he or she considers to be the single possible action. If a person of this type is teased or frightened, there are scant reserves of previous experience to call on, so emotion shoots straight through into ill-considered shouting or fury.

Clearly, such a narrowing is brought about by rigidly tight grouping. Religious and political bigotry are the results of such closeness, and so is the personal inadequacy of many thousands of people who have never been given the space and the richness of experience in which to develop the full potential of their response to it. Forcefulness is all that matters.

There is another and equally fundamental effect of over-crowding which must be considered, and that is the intermingling of awareness. People who share in a close grouping usually share also in the attitudes and opinions of that group. We tend to see this as voluntary, undertaken as a conscious agreement with the group's views, and this may be true in the case of joining a body such as Greenpeace or The Howard League for Penal Reform. There are, however, far more intrinsic groupings of which we are hardly aware. The family is the most fundamental group, taking a view of life which is intimately understood by all its members; in a "close" family, arguments are detailed ones centred round specific actions rather than disagreements on underlying assumptions. Social caste, however, underlies the family, as do occupations, levels of education and geographical location, and all these exercise a powerful sense of where one belongs.

Membership of these large groupings is often not conscious, much less chosen, but it colours the awareness of each individual with its own particular shared perception. Conventions of opinion become established within the group and are accepted by the members as truth. Casual overhearing of conversation reveals a multitude of such received opinions.

"People can get jobs if they really want to."
"A clip round the ear doesn't do kids any harm."
"Darling, *really* - what *do* you look like?"
"Books is boring."

These statements conjure up a vision of the kind of person who would make them, even though the particular speaker is quite unknown. In other words, they are representative of a group outlook. The words used by members of one group to describe another group say more about the describer than the described. It is the young and contemptuous who will refer to the old as "crumblies", and the middle-aged and impatient who will call children "brats". The difference between "an associate", "a friend", and "a mate" are not merely differences of degree but of attitude. "Yes, sir?" recognises the class gradient of the server and the served, whereas "Yes?" either resents it or is unaware of it. The words and phrases are selected in accordance with the outlook of the group to which the speaker feels him or herself to belong.

This feeling of "belonging" is caused partly by the communal pre-digesting of phenomena, but also by the intermingling of the sensory "root-system" with that of the neighbouring group members. This causes all experience to seem shared, with a high consensus of agreement as to its nature. Once this sharing is accepted as the normal state of things, the idea of being alone and outside the group is a frightening one which fills the individual with a fear of inadequacy. Conversely, a person who comes into the group with a well-developed creative capacity will find tightly-knit group membership intolerably constricting.

Here, the group acts as an impediment to the creative person's cycle of experience-use, because its network of much more closely-related cycles is interposed. The group itself will regard a creative incomer as an irritant, for his or her lack of conformity to the accepted patterns of thought will be disturbing. The immediate response will be to try and bring the new individual into line with the group's network. If this succeeds, the incomer will have to adjust and "fit in", even if this means abandoning the previous wider thought-cycles for the sake of conformity. If it does not succeed, the newcomer's creative cycle will remain undiminished, and he or she will exert a strong influence on the group, or remain outside it.

People capable of having such an effect are referred to as "natural leaders" if their influence is thought to be beneficial. If it is not, then they are called "disruptive elements". In either case, a strong sense of the self as an experiencer of life underlies the impact they are able to make. Our failure to recognise and understand this fact is the direct cause of much criminality.

Close grouping is popular with organisers. From their point of view, a biddable, undissenting mass is a desirable thing; it functions smoothly, as a single unit. In some circumstances, it seems in truth to *be* a single unit. Minnows in a stream turn as one thing. There are no confusions and collisions, for they all turn at the same instant. A flock of birds will do the same thing in the sky. Individually, they are able to build nests and find food and rear young, but collectively they have a shared awareness. A colony of bees has what bee-keepers know as "the hive mind"; it acts as a single entity composed of its particle bees. The hive organises its nourishment and decides when to rear queen cells and when to replicate itself by dividing off a new swarm.

With this in mind, we can see that ultra-tight groupings are only the opposite extreme from individuality in a limited sense, for they are capable of a shift of character which converts them into a unity. In this state, they exist as a collective self. From this point, the compression

29

The tight group is in fact inherently unstable, behaving sometimes as a collection of individuals and sometimes as a single transcending unity, just as a photon behaves sometimes as a particle and sometimes as an energy wave. The two states co-exist as constantly-fluctuating potential. Humans do not often move into the state of collective unity, but when they do, individual judgment is suspended, taken over by the "hive mind" of the group. The rhythmically-chanting Nazi rallies leap instantly to mind, and there is something of the same quality about the frenzy of football supporters. Warriors have always gone through the rituals of pre-battle bonding through dancing and chanting. Hallucinogens serve a useful purpose in subduing the individual awareness in favour of a sense of "togetherness", which is why alcohol plays such a vital part in preparation for combat. The tot of rum before engaging the enemy has ancient ancestors, as has the lager of the lager-lout.

A very different manifestation of collective unity in close groups may be the ability to know things about members of the group without any apparent physical means of communication. In the case of "second sight" so frequently testified to in the Scottish Highlands, for instance, the background was a closely-linked family system with little out-breeding. People who are strongly linked because they live through mutual support in isolated places seem able to know what is happening to each other without the need for physical communication.

Twins often have this ability to a marked extent, and many people confess to a sense of irrational alarm or distress at the moment of an accident to a family member far away.

Fundamental insecurity sends us towards groups, and reason would have it that a group becomes more secure with increasing tightness. The Army is the most obvious example of this. It is the nearest human equivalent of a bee-hive, with every component person allocated to a specific sub-division, named and valued according to the function carried out. Major, captain, sergeant, corporal - and the lowest grade is called private. Is this insignificant soldier nearest to being a private individual, and therefore less worthy? The corporal is clearly more corporate and the colonel in charge of a colony, the general in charge generally. The clothes, too, indicate the function within the group while seeking to suppress individuality. Crowns, chevrons, smooth cloth for officers but rough for ordinary soldiers, pacing sticks, shiny buttons, and for special occasions, a pomposity of bearskins and pipe-clayed spats. There is ferocious punishment for any individual who disturbs the autonomy of the group.

The intention of armies is to produce single-mindedness. Drill is intended to produce a squad of men who "move as one thing". An army, however, is commanded. Here lies the essential difference between natural groups such as bee-hives and human-directed groups such as armies, commercial firms, factories and schools. All of these are constructed for a specific purpose, and all are subject to a chain of command. The grouping is forced into tightness, not because of natural associativeness, but for the convenience of those in charge.

The difficulty here is that the "hive-mind" of the group may at any time decide that it does not want to obey those in charge. Sensing this, the response of the organisers is to intensify their authority over the group, often removing any privileges to individuals in the interests of forcing close-packed coherence. While there is still space for compression, this may work for a while, but eventually, the end of the cycle will be reached and the pressure within the group will explode it into a collection of individuals again. They will retain their unity of thinking for some time, even while rejoicing in what seems to be a new-found individuality, for a common delight in being free of the oppressor continues to bind them.

This is the classic state of revolution, where the inward pressure exerted by a dictatorship is reversed, and an outward movement towards what is seen as freedom begins.

Moving on through the cycle, the separation of the group continues, with increasing loss of connectedness between people. For a while, there will be a very constructive period of loose grouping, while the excitement of increasing freedom gives rise to new ideas. In Britain, this was seen clearly in the post-war years, when the country began to spread itself after the enforced unity and tightness of being a single faction in a combat. The Soviet Union, conversely, remained quite tightly grouped after its revolution, and is now continuing the outward movement so fast that it is in danger of by-passing the stage of being loosely grouped, joining the West in its social disconnectedness. Anarchy must become a serious threat before the necessary stress is created to trigger a reversal of the outward movement and a return towards constructive grouping. The cycle can thus be seen in terms of pressure. (Illustration 7 next page)

There is an obvious parallel with the laws of physics. Impossibility is approached when pressure becomes too great or too little; there will be explosion or implosion.

Between the extremes there is a condition of stasis. In terms of grouping, this optimum state arrives when each individual within the group derives the maximum benefit from group membership. Returning to the concept of the human creative function as a cycling of experience, it can be seen that each organism needs to be "in touch" with others, so as to have free access to their output of phenomena. If there is too much space, it is hard to reach this output. If there is too little, then creativity is limited by overcrowding.

Having identified this optimum state, the problem is to retain it. Looking at the diagram of expanding and contracting groups, it seems that there must constantly be a movement either towards compression or expansion. Half way between the two extremes, there is an identical state of loose grouping, but even so, it is moving inward or outward according

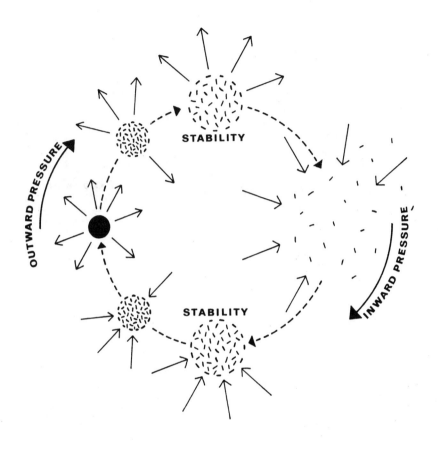

STABILITY

OUTWARD PRESSURE

INWARD PRESSURE

STABILITY

Illustration 7

to the side of the circle on which it is situated. Are we helplessly caught in a cycle which turns from anarchy to dictatorship and back again? I think not.

There can be a linking connection which is not shown on the diagram. One can imagine a second hoop, coming "towards" the reader (and disappearing behind the page) which joins the the midway points of stability. Like the ring which spans the spinning disc of a gyroscope, such a connecting circle works in a different, unchanging plane, exactly balanced between the extremes. Where it intersects with the disc, it will feel the influence of the move towards tightening or loosening, and some

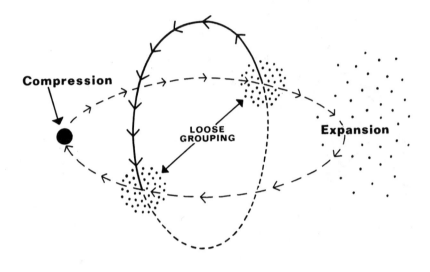

Compression

LOOSE
GROUPING

Expansion

Illustration 8

particles of its grouping will be pulled away by the spin. Even within stable mid-way groups, there will always be some joining and leaving, but unless it is completely overwhelmed, the collective coherence and character of a well-balanced group will not be affected. An orchestra, for instance, will see many changes of personnel during its life, but it can accommodate these without a threat to its existence. Only when too many players leave, or when the presence of a very powerful conductor or player imposes a restrictively tight convention on the group will real discomfort be felt - and it is then, of course, that instability sets in, with the orchestra collectively unhappy about its essential character.

For a group to have a long-lasting stability, all its members must feel reasonably comfortable. This means that they must be at the right distance from each other to have space for their own use of experience to be unimpeded, but that they are close enough to share in the common richness of the phenomena which all of them produce. In the case of an orchestra, it may be that many of the relationships are of purely musical value, but some will be based on shared humour or personal liking. The same thing is true of a school, and so it is obvious that a teacher who tries to tighten the grouping for disciplinary purposes is in fact pushing it towards instability. The acceptable density will be established by the children themselves, for the feeling-intelligence of each one of them will dictate how closely he or she can relate to the whole body. Such an optimum pre-condition encourages thinking which is, quite literally, "lateral".

Insecurity

When a baby is born, it loses the state of being an integral part of somebody else. Its first awareness is of a terrifying solitude. There is a sense of overwhelming loss which is never quite assuaged, for it lingers at the back of the mind of most adults, ready to express itself as self-doubt or embarrassment or fear.

The story of Adam and Eve's expulsion from the Garden of Eden owes its power to this general sense of having been pushed out of a previous existence which was perfect and effortless. In the Christian version, Eve is blamed for this disaster, and a universal guilt is thus set up which obscures the greater truth. The rejection which we suffer at birth, far from being some kind of punishment, is the mechanism through which our collective life continues.

The birth of a child can be seen for the purposes of this argument as exactly the same process as a flower bulb's propagation of itself by division. (Illustration 9 on following page)

The child at this stage has not developed reason or a general capacity for action to any great extent. It consists almost entirely of awareness and emotion, though feeling is also present, enabling the child to know that he or she is the person who weeps or who feeds and feels comfort. The senses and awareness are closely intermingled with the mother's, though there is no reason why another close person such as the father should not come into this intermingling as well.

Even in this early helplessness, the child cycles experience through its being, for if it does not do so, it cannot take in and use such phenomena as the mothers's voice and the comfort of her arms and, later, the presence of light and movement. These incoming experiences are part of the self. They are laid down as the beginnings of a growth of feeling and stored understanding which will establish a foundation for all further development. Without such a function, the child would be an inert emptiness approaching the state of vacuum. The sense of insecurity is the pressure exerted by this threatened vacuum which must fill itself with experience.

Even as a mature adult, every human being is vulnerable to an attack of feeling inadequate from time to time. There is a sense of being unable to find enough internal resources to deal with a situation. Seen mechanically, this can be expressed very simply as a difference in pressure.

"That shrinking feeling" is a perfectly accurate description of what is happening. When the creative processing of experience is reduced, the internal pressure of the organism drops. If it is a flexible unit, soft-walled because it is young or not "tough", it will simply contract, though this contraction reduces the overall capacity of the organism to do anything. If it is strong-walled and strong-willed, the difference in pressure will set up stress, pushing in on the feeling process. Continued input through the senses will build up in the awareness and cause an increase in emotion which the reduced feeling-activity cannot handle. Consequently, the state of raw emotion rises to be closer to the area of reason.

The effects are well known. Irritability bursts out in some cranky piece of reasoning, or a rising tide of unhappiness floods through the feeling process and overwhelms reason itself. Acute depression, where the sufferer is incapable of any action at all, can be seen as a complete inundation of the system in emotion. If it penetrates through reason into general action, the result can only be an output of emotion-loaded phenomena which will cycle round for re-ingestion. If no other input is supplied, this self-devouring may end in self-destruction.

Depression is experienced in circumstances where access to a rich input of experience is denied. It is the product of deprivation and boredom. Where there is nothing to be aware of except the things which are causing suffering, then awareness itself becomes an intolerable torment which must be ended.

Avoidance of this disaster is therefore the most primary need of the organism. A healthy throughput of experience-using is the only way to maintain an equilibrium. An enforced increase in this activity results in the more easily understood stress of overwork, which can be seen as too high an internal pressure. In either case, insecurity acts as the underlying motive force. Its threat of inadequacy is like the drop in pressure produced by a vacuum cleaner to cause a travelling current of air through itself. In the case of the living organism, the instinct to maintain a comfortable level of activity, neither boring nor over-demanding, is almost akin to a primary law of physics. It is obvious from the vacuum cleaner analogy that the pressure-gradient dictates the speed at which air passes through the mechanism. This underlying principle is true of all engines. A cylinder from which the air is withdrawn suffers a drop in pressure and the "instinct" of nature is to fill it with whatever is available. In the case of the internal combustion engine, it is filled with a petrol-and-air mixture which is compressed and ignited, and in the case of the human experiencing-mechanism, it is filled with phenomena which are then used in work of an expressive nature. This work may take the form of routine activity or commerce or art, just as a car's engine may propel the car slowly up a rutted lane or fast along a motorway - the harnessing of its energy is immaterial. But, in the case of the human and the mechanical functioning alike, there must be an adequate supply of fuel.

At the beginning of a child's life there is no shortage of experiential fuel. A baby is so obviously insecure that it is given warmth and cuddling and food unstintingly. It is interesting to notice, however, that babies in countries where they are carried with the mother all the time are hardly ever heard to cry, whereas babies lying alone in prams cry frequently. In the West, children are less easily integrated into adult life, for the structures of our civilisation were designed as a superimposition on nature rather that as a part of it.

Most parents, however, retain a strong instinct to protect and cherish their children and this, together with a pleasure in their existence, tends to provide a background of interest and stimulation during the early years. Most Western toddlers live in a plethora of toys and games and amusing objects. All this is used by the child to lay down the first stores of experience and understanding, but its demand for further supplies does not stop.

At this point, many parents begin to feel the child as a strain on their mental resources. "Go and play with your toys," a mother will say, and the child responds with, "They're boring." He or she is asking for activity, but a busy mother cannot always stop what she is doing, and she is often unable to integrate the child into her work, so she has to fend him off in some way. She will give him a packet of crisps or switch on the television. Up to a point, these diversions work well enough, but the child's need for first-hand experience is not being adequately satisfied, and his demands will continue.

Here, the child comes up against the limitations of the parents themselves. Many people have during their own childhood accepted that boredom and routine are inevitable, and have scaled down their creative functioning to be comfortable within these restrictions. Both school and employment reinforce the need for this scaling-down in the interests of compliance. To such people, the demands of a child seem presumptuous, and the constant questioning becomes irritating, for it seeks to provoke an increased output of creative energy, causing a sense of inadequacy and exhaustion.

The response of the parents is often to try and reduce the child's creative cycling of experience to match with their own. Nobody complains about an under-active child, and these are praised as "being no bother", but the hyper-active child, on the other hand, is now a recognised pathological case. "Junk" foods, with their additives and preservatives, play a part in such a child's metabolism, but the fact that the child has been given them is in itself indicative of a desire to fend off and placate. The message is clear - that passivity is better than activity, compliance better than argument. The good child is the one who causes no trouble.

Pre-school play groups can supply children with a broadening of experience, but at three or four years old, children already vary considerably in their ability to benefit from it. Some have an intact and confident need for experience and will be full of questions and opinions. Others, whose cycle of experience-using is not so well-established, will want to return to the mother, who is still the main supply of security. The third and most difficult group consists of the truculent, complaining ones, for whom everything is someone else's fault. These are the blamers, and there are thousands of them, both children and adults.

Blaming is a curious mechanism. It works in almost the same way as depression in that there is a great discomfort due to the sense of inadequacy. An awareness of this discomfort is shaped by the feeling-process and made manifest as lethargy of movement and constant grumbling, but whereas the depressed person knows that these are of his or her own making (and feels even worse for having made them) the blamer mistakes their origin. Instead of recognising that the grumbles and accusations are self-made, he or she thinks they are external phenomena, originating from an objective appraisal of the situation. This conviction reinforces the original state of truculence and can produce hysterical irrationality in which the outrageousness of the world seems intolerable. Emotion boils straight through the system, pushing the feeling-process aside and forcing reason into a contorted rebuilding of the way things seem to be.

Blamers are typically people who have no time for feeling and who pride themselves on being strong. Their contempt for the feeling process may well have been laid down by parents who themselves admired strength, condemning tears as "babyish". The need for experience may have been filled only by a "tough" father who, though terrifying, could command admiration because he was not boring. Such a confusion produces a child who will blame the meek, unterrifying mother for anything irksome rather than disturb the linked admiration and fear which he feels for his father. Boys are much more prone to this distorted mental pattern than girls, for they fall prey more commonly to a suppression of their feelings in childhood. They tend to replicate the behaviour of the father, for the habit of blaming is ingrained and it must find a willing recipient. The adult blamer is apt to claim that he "needs" a drink rather than simply wanting one. He also needs someone to be held responsible for his pain and will grumble endlessly about the Government or the boss or the Council. Such bodies, however, lack immediacy, and a much more fundamental scapegoat is the wife who, because she tries to please him, will accept his blame compliantly, shutting down her own creative cycle to a state of dulled endurance and tacitly reinforcing his illusions. The children of such a couple will find it hard to steer a way between brutality and humiliation.

Finding this balance is vitally important, for it is the equivalent of achieving a smooth "tick over" in an engine. When a load is added to it, more energy is called for, and any imbalance is increased. An engine in this unbalanced condition can run itself to destruction.

Primary schools generally acknowledge the importance of the child's creative functioning, although this is partly because it is impossible at this stage to teach without reference to it. Children have few skills except the ability to see and hear, touch and feel, and so when they enter school these are the abilities which must be used. Once literacy and numeracy are established to some degree, the skills of the senses are progressively abandoned in favour of more theoretical knowledge. It is only in the very young that self-expression forms an integral part of learning.

As the child grows older, its performance is increasingly evaluated in terms of correct or incorrect answers. The devising of alternative possibilities or the pointing out of flaws in the received wisdom results in disapproval. The expression of personal feeling is usually irrelevant to the field of study and memory is of far more value than conjecture. As Michael Forsyth said in December 1990, speaking as Scottish Minister for Education, "We must make sure our children are as well educated as those in Germany or Japan, to give us a skilled work-force." Or, in other words, to be useful to the system.

From the child's point of view, there is a progressive withdrawal of interest in him or her as a person. For the few who will go on to higher education, the work itself can supply a cycling of experience which is rewarding. They can develop relatively smoothly, their minds fully engaged with what they are doing, and since they are the "successes" of the school system, they have the added bonus of approval.

For the others - and, except for Greece, Britain has the lowest percentage in Europe of children entering further education - the sense of withdrawal of interest is often acute. Their value, if any, will be as part of the workforce. For many, even that shred of self-respect is not available. A watered-down version of the academic curriculum does not touch their perception of what they are.

Insecurity at this point is at its maximum. The young person wants to be valued, so it seems essential to appear to be independent and capable. Parents belong to the old, discarded days of dependence, so they, too, must be cast off, even though their support and help may be desperately needed. If the young person is a blamer, the parents are the first in the firing-line to be held responsible for the aridity of the situation, and if, as frequently happens, his or her parents are also blamers, the accusations will be reciprocated, and a situation of great hostility and unhappiness will arise.

Teenagers often feel acutely aware of being alone. The wail of "You don't understand!" is familiar to many parents, as is the experience of seeing their child become a member of a group of grotesquely-dressed and uncommunicative layabouts, laughing at obscure private jokes, eating a lot of food and giving no satisfactory explanation for staying out late. The behaviour seems calculated to provoke a parental outburst.

This grouping is a response to the mounting insecurity which worsens in the upper years of the Secondary school, where there is often scant affection or even civility between teachers and pupils. Bonding into tight groups with a shared style is a defence mechanism, for such groups build up a cycling of common awareness which helps to exclude unwelcome phenomena such a teacher's scolding or a parent's protests. They provide a sense of identity and self-respect within themselves so any attacks from outside can be withstood. There is even a certain sense of triumph in demonstrating to the other members of the group that such attacks have lost their power to hurt, which is why teenage behaviour tends to be so provocative. It is a self-testing of far more significance than the irrelevant ritual of school examinations, which seem devised for the express purpose of causing humiliation.

Teen-age groups are short-lived, fragile things despite their intensity. Members enter the workforce and give up the struggle to express their true identity because they recognise that the style in which they were expressing it marks them as immature and unacceptable. Others fail to enter the workforce in any conventional way, and either accept the recognised status of being unemployed or find some alternative in the form of legal or illegal ways of surviving. Much more important in personal terms is the sexuality which comes to the fore at about this time, with its fascinating promise of a new duality.

The timing is mechanically perfect. At the lowest point of ebbing confidence, when even the teenage group is proving to be an illusory defence against the sense of isolation and inadequacy, a new possibility makes itself felt within the most personal and intimate awareness. Not since the forgotten state of pre-birth has there been such a feeling of acceptance and completion. As a device for the reproduction of the species, it could not be better. In human terms, it offers a promise which can seldom be fulfilled, for the sex drive, like any other kind of hunger, is an emptiness which seeks to fill itself but constantly occurs again. A starving person will eat anything which comes to hand, and a desperately isolated teenager will snatch at the fulfilment which offers itself, regardless of its suitability.

Among well-fed people with a healthy appetite, the provision of food is a creative act, balancing flavours and textures with discriminating judgment. Similarly, in people who have a well-established acceptance of themselves as users of experience, the sexual act becomes a skilled and subtle pleasure. It is always powered by an element of need, just as a delight in food requires some degree of hunger - hence the ritual wishing of "bon appetit" - but the confidence and self-control of the good cook or the good lover raise the satisfying of need to a form of artistry. Here, insecurity is transcended.

In a truly rewarding relationship, both partners must function as complete individuals, able to use experience in their own terms. Where this is not established, the demands made are too heavy, for they resemble the dependence of babyhood. The jealous husband wants the complete security of what he sees as the whole of his wife's being, and the girl who says, "I feel incomplete without him", speaks of inadequacy rather than love.

Freud saw this desire to re-enter a state of duality from an exclusively male viewpoint, as a dynamic attitude of the child to the mother. His concept of "infant sexuality" should, I believe, be reversed. "Sexual infancy" is closer to the basic need which insecurity brings about. Certainly, for the female, the idea of love is associated with comfort and acceptance and unreserved sharing - which is why rape is such a violating abuse. Few women enjoy sex unless it offers cuddling and affection. The very language of sexual intimacy tends to express a re-experiencing of infancy, with its half-articulate murmurings and nuzzlings. John Osborne is accurate about this in his play, "Look Back in Anger", where his lovers use the nursery language of bears and squirrels within their private duality. Outside it, as they full well know, lies the jungle, for Jimmy Porter is deeply insecure. He in fact creates the jungle, for he is a classic "blamer", and his beloved Alison, who is his world, is also seen as the source of all his pain.

Many such relationships are inexplicable to dismayed parents and friends of the couple concerned. Often, the dismay is shared by the partners themselves in moments of clarity, but the illusion of shared identity is so powerful that it transcends reason.

Taken to its natural conclusion, the need for sexual sharing will result in the birth of a child. This, for the mother, is the genuine sharing to which her insecurity has urged her. It is a creative act of the first order, and it brings about a new and slightly dismissive attitude to the sexual need she felt previously. Partnerships founded on mutual insecurity often start to fail at this point, though parents who have confidence in themselves as well as in each other will be enriched by the new life they have made together.

The cycle begins again, with the new-born child aware only of what the adults who care for it can supply. It inherits insecurity as an inescapable bequest. If it is lucky, it will grow up to understand that this gift is the best thing which any fairy godmother could give. Insecurity produces the initial sense of threatened vacuum which starts up the need for experience. It can be relaxed into as the only certainty, for all the apparently invincible structures of human making are ultimately fallible. The only reality is that one is aware of experience, and within this is such limitless wonder that it takes a lifetime to try to express it. Some people are more aware than others, just as some are taller or stronger, and so some have the capacity to be a "giant" among creators, like Bach or Leonardo; this does not prevent others from engaging in the same activities any more than Olympic athletes prevent the less intensely-trained from enjoying a country walk or a gentle jog. To live is

Poets were the scientists of the ancient world and in the new scientific view of the universe there is, alas, no place for them.

Brian Branston
The Lost Gods of England.

Time and Experience

So far, the bulb-like diagram of the human being as a creative user of experience has been shown floating on the blank page, with no reference to anything else except the surrounding bodies and the phenomena which arrive in the awareness. The view is an external one, designed with the same purpose as an anatomical drawing; no attempt is made to define the way in which the body lives. The structure is laid bare, but in order to understand its intrinsic nature, it must be sensed from the inside as well as seen from the outside. Since every human being looks out from within the self, this is a natural process.

To establish the internal view, one need only ask the question, "How do I know I am alive?"

There could be many answers, but they are all to do with sensation. I am holding this book, seeing these words, feeling the chair I sit in, hearing the traffic outside the window or the ticking of a clock. Descartes declared that he knew he was alive because he thought. "Cogito ergo sum" has lodged in many minds as a reasonable statement, but in fact it is a deceptive one. To cogitate is a secondary activity, an organisation of the material which has arrived in the mind through the awareness, and to mistake it for a fundamental state leads to a belief that the structures of one's own mind are objectively real. This is a misunderstanding which has had disastrous results in the last couple of hundred years.

The accurate answers to the question of knowing one is alive are all descriptions of present experience. Holding, seeing, feeling, hearing....all these words describe an immediate awareness of the state which we call Now.

Part of the mind can imagine the future or remember the past, but awareness of these things happens in the present, as does everything we do - and yet the state of Now perplexes us, for it seems like a knife edge, an insubstantial turning-point between the past and the future. A moment is no sooner realised than it has gone. We appear to be living in an onward-rolling temporariness, pushed along by the ever-accumulating past into the unknown future.

Seeing the present in this way is the result of imagining time to be an on-going line which carries us helplessly with it. Such a view increases the sense of isolation and insignificance, for it puts no value on awareness, regarding it as a fleeting and untrustworthy noticing of a state which is itself fleeting. As a result, we put our faith in structures which seem strong enough to defy time's erosion of our self-confidence. "Safe as houses", we say, revealing how we want to reinforce our belief that we can be powerful.

The passage of time can be seen in a very different way if we abandon preconceptions and trust to the evidence of our senses. One can progress by easy stages from one view to the other, beginning with the well-established notion of time as a continually moving stream on which we are carried. A leaf floating on a stream moves with it, but it does not move in relation to the area of water on which it sits. At that point, there is stillness. In exactly the same way, we do not move in relation to time. Our awareness is rooted in the Now, which is our connection with the body of time, however we choose to see it. (Ilustration 10 on following page)

Obviously, we cannot alter our position in the time-flow, otherwise we would slither from today to yesterday or from this afternoon to tomorrow morning *in our actual experience*, which is of course impossible.We have to remain within our own state of continuing Now. There is no movement of time through the feeling-process, for it is the setting in which we are fixed.

We have a strong sensation of the passing of time, but this is caused by the circling of experience through the consciousness. At the beginning of life, there is no confusion about this. A baby knows only the rhythms of its own body - hunger and the expelling of waste, the beating of the heart and the moving in and out of breath. It has no concept of time. When it begins to store the memory of previously-experienced events, the baby will begin to sense that there is a rhythm to them. They have happened before. To understand this is to lay down the first awareness of one's own cycling of experience. Previous wakings and comfortings have happened at roughly similar intervals. Crying begins to seem connected with the arrival of comfort, but the baby still has no idea of what time it is.

With the development of the senses, more phenomena begin to be taken in. Light can be seen, and after a while, it is associated with a memory of having seen it before. Lightness comes and stays for a while, then goes away again, in a slow rhythm. The period when it is light begins to be experienced as a repeated manifestation which will later on be identified as a "day". Such experiencing and classifying still has nothing to do with a concept of time; it is related entirely to the movement of phenomena through the awareness.

Within the marker posts which are set up like bar lines in music by the recurrence of day and night, a certain amount of activity can be fitted. A bar of music may contain a flurry of semiquavers or a single long note, or it may be silent. Similarly, a day may be filled with a lot of activities or it may be spent in gazing at the sea, or it could pass in sleep and contain no activity at all. The person who wants to put a lot of action into any

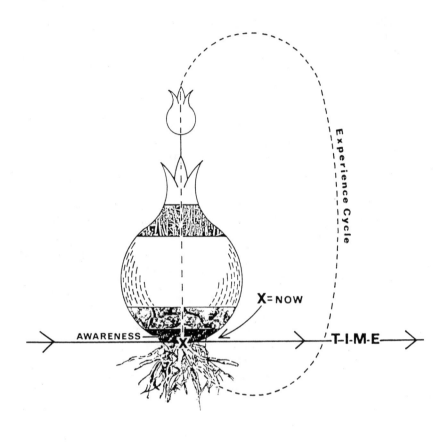

AWARENESS

X = NOW

T-I-M-E

Experience Cycle

Illustration 10

period of time will have to work hard - that is to say, speed up his or her cycle of experience-using.

When the experience-cycle is devoid of stimulation, it hardly moves at all, so its owner is conscious of little except a sense of extreme slowness. Ten minutes spent in the enforced idleness of waiting for a train can seem to be a very long time, and yet, if those ten minutes were spent in drinking a cup of coffee with an amusing friend, there could be a danger of missing the train because the time had slipped past so quickly. In both cases, the word "time" is misapplied. It is experience, not time, which is happening slowly or fast.

It may be argued that there could be no sense of tedium or of hurry without an underlying sense of how we feel comfortable with time. Once we emerge from the unquestioning babyhood acceptance of Now, we increasingly glance at the clock. "Time flies", we say or, conversely, "Time drags. Roll on five o'clock." The feeling that time is a flexible thing seems to be a very real one. There could be a rational explanation for this. Anyone will understand it who has seen a squad of soldiers turn in what is known as a "right wheel".

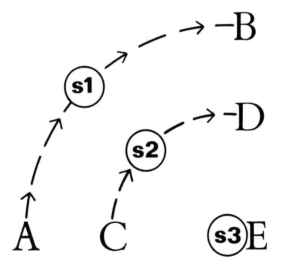

Illustration 11

Soldier no 1 has to lengthen his stride in order to get from A to B, whereas soldier 2 need make no adjustment. Soldier 3 will have to take a few steps "on the spot" while the others swing round him and realign in their new direction.

Even the non-mathematical will readily see that the distance from A to B is greater than the distance from C to D.

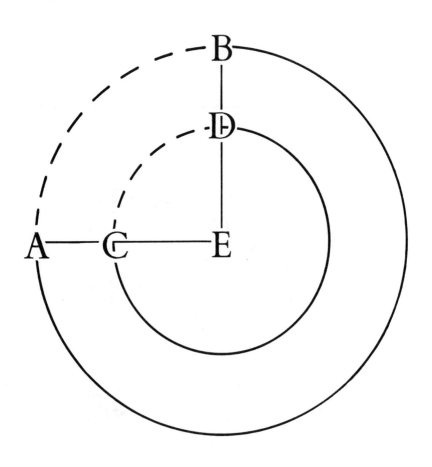

Illustration 12

The same thing is true of any circle. If the circle is a rotating disc, anything placed at A or B will travel further during a single rotation than a thing placed at C or D, whereas a thing placed at E will not travel at all, but simply rotate on its axis. The larger the circle, the faster the movement at its edge.

Quite separately, it could be imagined that a circle's actual speed of turning can be increased by mechanical means, like the wheels of an accelerating car. A fast-turning small wheel could have a velocity at its edge which is the same as that of a slower-turning larger wheel, in which case the two will mesh together comfortably. This is, of course, the principle of gearing.

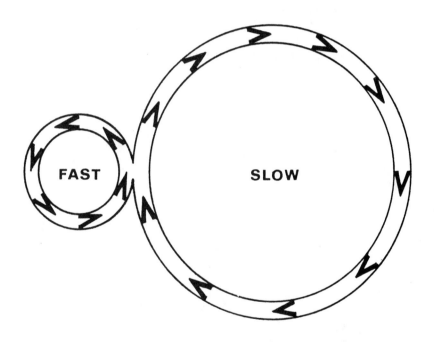

Illustration 13

The human-experience cycle obeys the same mechanical law. Our acceleration of mental activity can happen in one (or both) of two ways; we can increase effort, thus speeding up the cycle's rate of turning, or we can develop the size of the experience-cycle itself, which will give it the potential for faster speed at its outer edge. The implications of these different approaches in human terms are considerable, but for the moment the main concern is the mechanical function.

The self, as we have seen, must remain firmly connected to time through the joining-point of Now, for this is our continuing state, the foundation of our existence. When this connection is severed, our relationship with time is broken, and we change into potentiality rather than actuality, in the state called death, leaving the body behind to be subject to the working of time. The person, being no longer in its own Now, become Then, a thing of the past.

If we see the cycle of experience as a wheel rather than a rough circle as it appeared in the early diagrams, we can also see how its awareness can connect through the point of Now with another circle which we can think of as time. This is not very different from the picture of the creative cycle as rooted in the time-stream, for inter-relating cogs serve the same purpose as roots, supplying a connection.

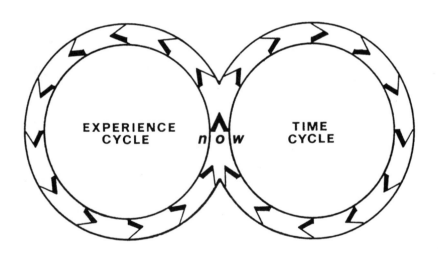

Illustration 14

52

Where the two circles rotate at the same speed and remain the same size, they will relate to each other without stress, and the Now remains constant.

If the size of the experience-cycle increases through personal development, the edge of it will increase its speed. The same thing will happen if the cycle is driven faster. In order to retain contact with the time-wheel through the meshing-point of Now, some adjustment must be made.

Time cannot cycle any faster, for it is the constant medium against which we measure all other movement. The only adjustment it can feasibly make is to grow bigger. If we accept that there is no limitation to time in terms of size, then there is a universal adjustment which can easily be made. A larger or faster-turning experience-cycle only needs to move fractionally further from time's centre in order to encounter a faster-moving surface. It is an infinitely variable gearing similar to that of a cone related to a disc.

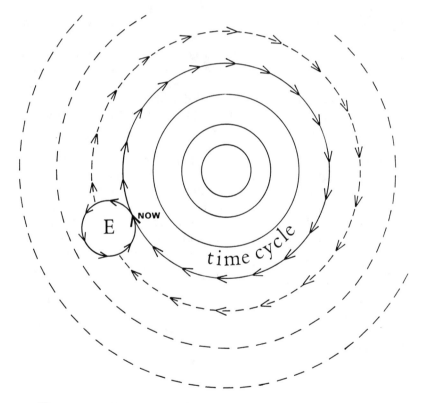

E = *experience cycle*

Ilustration 15

Since the point at which the self finds its Now is unimaginably far from time's centre, the progress of time appears to be straight, just as the earth's surface appears to be flat. Within the idea of circularity, there is a sense of being contained, and of seamless continuance, whereas the concept of straightness implies that there must be an end and a beginning, and that the onward progress has no significant relationship to humanity.

It is for this reason of "how things seem" that the conceptualising of a time structure is of any value. We need to perceive that our existence is not irrelevant to the existence of everything else, and the idea of time as a linear progress can give no such assurance. So far, the projected model of time as a rotating circle has been seen in very simple two-dimensional terms, but even so, it begins to be obvious that there are, from any individual's point of view, two centres. One is the centre of the time circle, where the spin must come to a point of stillness, and the other is the centre of the self's experience cycle. Here again, there is stillness.

The mechanical model shows that awareness and its connection to time through the point of Now must be at the outer edge of the self. Awareness, in computer jargon, would be called the "interface", standing between the inner self and the outside world. The centre, however, is by definition as far from the edge as it can get. The inference in human terms is clear. The centre of one's being is not the same thing as the awareness. Returning to the diagram of the self as a biological organism, we can see that this centre is the "I" which is served by the senses but is not of the senses. If I feel, I know that I am the I which does the feeling. (Illustration 16 on following page)

The still centre of the self is not only as far as possible from awareness, but also at a significant distance from reason. It cannot be seen or heard or touched, and neither can it be demonstrated to exist in rational terms. Reason, therefore, tends to claim that no such centre exists, and the outward senses likewise can find no evidence for it. Feeling, however, encloses and protects the central self, and this is the only area which has direct contact with it. Deep at the centre of our feeling is the indefinable thing which we call the soul. Because we cannot understand it, we feel faintly embarrassed to talk about it, for this age is concerned almost exclusively with the rational, and tries hard to ignore the evidence of feeling. To admit that the soul, rather than the brain, is the centre of human existence, runs counter to the structure of importance which we have built up, but it is an admission which must be made before any constructive understanding of creativity can be achieved.

54

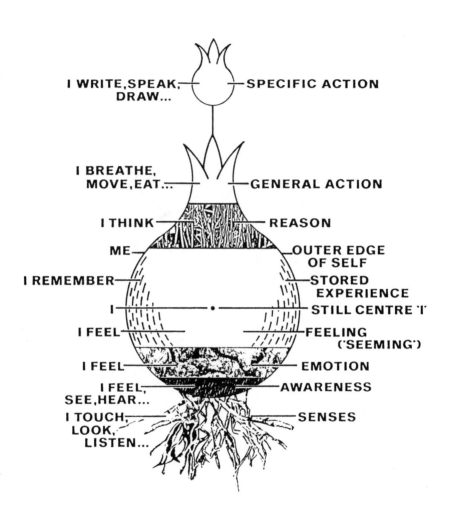

I WRITE, SPEAK, DRAW... — SPECIFIC ACTION

I BREATHE, MOVE, EAT... — GENERAL ACTION

I THINK — REASON

ME — OUTER EDGE OF SELF

I REMEMBER — STORED EXPERIENCE

I — STILL CENTRE 'I'

I FEEL — FEELING ('SEEMING')

I FEEL — EMOTION

I FEEL, SEE, HEAR... — AWARENESS

I TOUCH, LOOK, LISTEN... — SENSES

Illustration 16

55

All this he saw, for one moment breathless and intense, vivid on the morning sky; and still, as he looked, he lived; and still, as he lived, he wondered.

Kenneth Grahame
The Wind In The Willows

The Necessary Goat

Children are immensely adept researchers into the nature of things, because they start with no preconceptions.

"What's that?"

"It's a sheep."

"Oh."

The child stares at the animal and sees the thin, hair-covered legs and the shaggy mass of wool and the face with its Roman nose and impassive eyes, the jaws moving rapidly. Later, the sheep will be reduced to a category; a provider of wool and meat, or else a symbol of sheep-like qualities. The open curiosity of childhood is something which creative people manage to retain, but for most of us, it is steadily eroded and replaced by classification. The experience of encountering the sheep is not considered to be of any particular importance.

Looking again at the "bulb" diagram, the difference between classification and strongly-realised experience can be seen very clearly. (Illustration 17 on following page)

In *A*, the sheep has been taken in completely, to become part of the viewer's stored experience. As such, it can then be used as fuel for a picture or a poem, though further lookings will be needed to strengthen the reality. Such experience becomes stored reference. A shepherd will use it in great detail to compare one animal with another, and this is what enables him to know each ewe and lamb individually. Recognition comes from positively-realised experience.

In *B*, the sheep has only marginally been realised. The experience of seeing it is stored as an item called "sheep", but it has not been consciously felt or made part of the viewer. As an item of information, it is ready for use in whatever context is required, and this, in the vast majority of cases, is the preferred use for such material. The classification of information is considered more important than intensity of experience.

Because the purpose of classification is to establish a common ground of reference, it produces convention. The stored information usually arrives through the direction of other people because the manner of its storage is considered more important than the realising of it as a freely

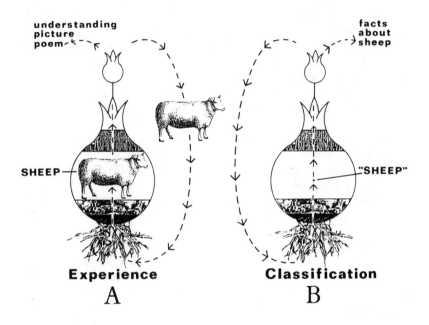

Illustration 17

undertaken experience. Therefore these storage patterns tend to have a similarity, and they give rise to common assumptions, not only in practical terms but in symbolic ones. Children learn to associate the sheep with marginal and hill farming, with New Zealand and, more recently, with the Common Agricultural Policy in Europe, but they also learn, in a much more subliminal way, that the sheep is a symbol of obedience and tractability. It is no accident that the sheep is a pervasive element in Christian teaching.

The Lord is my shepherd
Little lamb, who made them?
And we like sheep have gone astray.
He shall feed his flock.

To people of true spirituality, the sense of being in touch with a greater entity than the self is palpable, and the mysterious guidance which it implies is manifest in an enhanced breadth of choice, but the conventional significance of the sheep as a symbol does not touch on such mysteries. It is a debased and corrupted version of an exalted idea, so generally accepted that it becomes administratively useful. The virtue of the sheep suggests that those in charge of us know better than we do. To be good is to be compliant.

The establishment of this assumption is a basic principle in the current management of society. Schools are expected above all to instill obedience. If academic achievement follows, so much the better, but the prime criterion by which a school is judged is in the degree of order which it can impose. A neatly-dressed, quietly behaved body of children is more acceptable than an untidy rabble. It may be true that within the orderly group there is a lively and fulfilling process of learning at work, but it could equally be true of the untidy group. Superficial judgment does not make any attempt to assess these deeper values. The appearance of orderliness is in itself enough to assure the onlooker that the school system is an effective one. Such a judgment is usually perfectly correct, because all teaching must begin with a collecting-together of attentiveness - but the use made of the attentiveness does not enter into the assessment. In an ironic circularity, people respect a school which can command respect; the products of an authoritarian system are authorized to accept authoritarianism, and nothing else. Even such small anarchies as the calling of a member of staff by his or her first name provoke shakings of the head and mutterings of foreboding.

It is, in other words, the school *system* which is held to be important. Every child knows that it is the relationship with the teacher which really matters, but this does not enter into any recognised assessment of success, because we do not primarily think of people as experiencers but as performers. As such, their performance is expected to fit within the provided structure, and when it does not fit, then the structure is seen as threatened, and it will therefore be defended. A child whose behaviour is disruptive is seldom regarded as a sufferer who is finding the system difficult - on the contrary, the system is felt to be suffering from a difficult child. For this reason the ultimate sanction against a persistent offender is to bar him or her from coming to the school at all. This does nothing to solve the child's problems, but it protects the institution against the individual. Nonsensical judgments of this kind abound in society. A car parked in an offending position may have its wheels clamped, which means that the offence must be continued for several hours more while the car's owner is put to maximum inconvenience and expense by way of retribution. The purpose is devoid of practicality; it is designed purely to reinforce respect for the system. The same can be said for imprisonment, which is grotesquely inefficient and which serves only as a tangible reminder of the power of the state over the individual.

School initiates the process of anti-creativity which results in men and women being thought of as units rather than as free experiencers of life. The examination system requires that all children learn the same facts so that a common ground is established for assessment purposes. At least half the functioning of the human lies within the sphere of feeling rather than reason, and so does not lend itself to objective examination. It is therefore ignored. Our methods of assessment deal only with reason and the retention of facts. They have no means of evaluating the potential of a child with a broad base of awareness and a strong sense of his or her own self as a creative user of experience.

Creativity is usually regarded in much narrower terms. "We have Creativity on Friday afternoons", a Headmistress told me once. "The children are too tired by then to do any proper work." The attitude is distressingly common, and it debars the holder from the great richness of understanding which comes from direct experience. To be aware of a thing with complete openness is , as we have seen, to make that thing part of the self - but it also makes the self part of the outside world. It is an interaction of awareness and existence, and as such, it helps to dispel the sense of isolation and insignificance which lies at the base of the human psyche.

A young child can enter easily into such interactions; everyone has seen a toddler utterly absorbed in examining some newly-discovered object, unaware of being separate from it because of the total mingling of the object and the self. Some people retain a partial ability to achieve this mingling, though it is not encouraged in older children as it appears to be purposeless. At the end of a school day, such children tend to remember the details of what their teacher was wearing or what the class managed to produce as a diversion rather than the information which was imparted, unless the topic in hand happened to be one which presented a reality of its own which interested them. The erratic quality of their attention can be extremely irritating to their teachers.

"There are sheep", a Headmaster once told my daughter, "and there are goats. And you are a goat." It was meant as a reproof, and she was deeply hurt. Only much later, when she accepted her goat status as a fact of which she was not ashamed, could she admit that he spoke the truth.

The symbolism of the sheep-and-goats analogy is universally understood. With the sheep established as the preferred species, the goat represents the reject of the flock. The animal itself is regarded as hairy, smelly and anarchic. It is a very Western view, for in countless parts of the world, the goat enables humans to survive through it own tenacity, for it provides milk and cheese, meat and leather, in places where sheep could not live. The idea of the goat as an undesirable creature is a strange one, but it is so deeply ingrained in the western European value-system that its origins are worth investigating.

Religious education often ignores pre-Christianity even though the world's contemporary non-Christian religions are increasingly studied. The Biblical references to Paganism are seldom enlarged on, and many children assume that people were uncultured savages before the birth of Jesus of Nazareth. The Romans and the Greeks have some familiarity, largely because of their linguistic and historic effect on Europe, but there is virtually no teaching at all about the religion which prevailed here in the earlier centuries vaguely lumped together as "B.C.".

This religion was a Goddess-worshipping one, deeply rooted in a feeling that the nature of life is in itself sacred, and that birth is a recurring miracle which exemplifies it. There was not, at this time, any clear understanding of the connection between copulation and birth, so the female was seen as an autonomous creator, possessed of immense power. Naturally, an idea of a creator-spirit in abstract terms was also female, for the male was regarded as a light-weight, transient being, much loved and delighted in, but essentially impermanent. The impermanence was ritualised to a point where a young man who was particularly beloved of the priestesses was sacrificed annually. The pain of his loss was real, symbolising the willingness of the female to be used by the demands of life itself, no matter at what cost in terms of suffering.

With the understanding of the male role in conception and birth came a great fury. For centuries, men had not been able to see themselves as important. They had been marginal to the structure of female-held power (which, like all power, had begun to be abused) and now that they understood their sexual role and knew that a male act triggered the process of birth, they felt an enormous surge of anger and desire for retribution. What followed was the most important revolution of our entire history, and the effects of it are with us to this day.

The male revolution brought about a cataclysmic overthrow of the female-dominated religion which had ruled society for centuries. Like all revolutions, it was violent and brutal, and its guerrillas were bound together by the shared passion of a new faith. The Jewish male deity, Yahweh, already had a devoted following, but the New Testament chronicles the birth and life of the man who was to stand as a tangible link between humanity and God. The directness of the connection had enormous appeal, for it seemed to provide a religious reality which was new and exciting. The overthrow of mystery always has a powerful attraction for the man in the street, and the new Christianity appealed specifically to the man as a male. The resentment of female domination was given a triumphant outlet in the new belief that God was male and, furthermore, that all the ills in the world were the fault of the first woman. The story of the Garden of Eden is an ancient one, long pre-dating the birth of Christ, but is it only in the Biblical version that the loss of paradise is blamed on the disobedience of Eve. The male seizing of power was avid and ruthless. For the first time, children were called by the father's name rather than the mother's, and women were brought under strict control, their status demoted to that of a possession which the husband could treat as he liked.

With this new and deeply misogynistic religion came a turning-away from creativity as the basis of ordinary life. The ideas of the birth-giver and Pagan life-worship had been so entwined that they could not be separated; consequently, the explanation for the arrival of Jesus on the earth was a convoluted one, designed to avoid any indebtedness to female sexuality in its process. The Virgin Mary is a saintly and utterly sexless handmaiden of the Lord, quite different from ordinary women whose birth-giving remained a Pagan-tainted sin. Until quite recently, the service called "the churching of women" was held to purge a newly-delivered mother from the offence she had committed. Creativity became a specifically artistic activity carried out almost exclusively by males while the more general creativity of the female attitude was vigorously suppressed.

Creative expression, in the eyes of the early Christians, could only be accepted if it took the form of worship of the male God, which is why the great flowering of European music and painting is religious in character. Once it began to venture into the secular field, the concept of the artist as "Bohemian" and slightly outside the accepted centre of society began to be established. For women, creativity was strictly limited to the domestic skills. Intelligent women who showed signs of ability in healing or in psychological perspicacity were persecuted as witches, and it is interesting to note that their activities were always described as "heretical". The association with pre-Christian female power was not dead. Female creativity was not merely a secular crime, but a religious taboo.

It seems curious, in retrospect, that women accepted the new faith in such large numbers, and even more curious that they continue to embrace it. There was not, at first, much choice. Revolutions do not permit dissent. But there were more subtle ways in which Christianity dovetailed with female psychology. There had always been an element of willingly-undertaken suffering. The giving up of the cherished young lover, Tammuz, had been a ritual designed to demonstrate that women were prepared to suffer in the service of life. Because a certain degree of suffering is built in to female life in the processes of menstruation and childbirth, its endurance is an integral part of the female mind. The Christian interpretation was to make this suffering into an expiation of guilt, the inherited curse which Eve handed down to her daughters. There must have been, too, a certain ease in accepting the young man Jesus as the eternal sacrifice which replaced the annual agony of Tammuz. Since Tammuz himself had often been symbolised by an animal in the later Goddess years, there may even have been an awareness of decadence and

63

a faint shame that the sacrifice had become too easy. The agony of Christ fitted neatly into this shame as an outlet for sublimated suffering, particularly as the sharing in it promised forgiveness and redemption. But underlying all hope was the basic demand imposed by Christianity for an admission of guilt and, more importantly, for a recognition that the individual sinner is helpless within it. The prayer for forgiveness is perpetual, and never fully answered. Passivity, then, becomes a virtue. Action, unless undertaken as a direct act of worship, must always seem worldly and faintly sacrilegious.

Despite all efforts to abolish the Goddess cult of life-worship, the idea refused to die completely. It survived in Greece (and thence in the rest of the world) as the god Pan, bearded and horned and irreverent. His symbolic power has always had a nod of recognition, for Pantheism, even now, continues to be a strand interwoven with the major religions, and the current Green movement is instinctively veering towards a full-circle return to it. Through the figure of Pan, we are brought face to face with the symbolism of the goat.

Pan personifies the life-force which had been the basis of the Goddess religion and which was so hated and resented by the male revolutionaries. The tactics of attack always concentrate on belittling the enemy and reducing it to an insignificant and absurd symbol. Adolf Hitler's small moustache and drooping cow-lick of hair probably did more to undermine his credibility than any amount of anti-Nazi propaganda - to this day, a finger laid across the upper lip and an arm raised in stiff salute are recognised as a sketch of Fascism. Similarly, Pan, with his goat legs and horns, was a suitably trivial representation of life-worship in the eyes of the new power-holders. He was easily derided.

With Christianity, however, came a further problem. The new God was a perfect being, embodying the absolute goodness of the divine Father. He did not encapsulate both good and evil as the old Pagan matriarchy had done, and so there was a need for an opposing figure to embody absolute evil. Pan was the obvious candidate. He already symbolised the overthrown and discredited religion, and it was an easy matter to give him a scaly skin and a barbed tail, and to replace his musical pipes by a three-pronged fork with which to torment the souls who roasted in Hell. Pan was changed into the Devil.

The connection between the idea of the goat and of the Devil remains very strong. Goatish qualities of independence and scepticism are only welcomed among people whose membership of the ruling elite is unquestionable. Until very recently, it has been virtually impossible for women to have any political or religious influence - the refusal of most churches to entertain the idea of a female clergy is a direct manifestation of the ancient hostility to the power which Christianity usurped, and in which it is still not entirely secure. The continuing suspicion of the idea that life as its own self is holy results in a great caution about whose opinion may be listened to. The opinion of men is, even now, often considered to be weightier than that of women, and among men, the important are heard more attentively than the unimportant. There is no reason why this should be so, except that the structure which was built during the years of the male revolution still stands. It is a cage in which life is imprisoned and on which man stands.

Our attitude to children is determined absolutely by the rigidity of this cage. A child who is fascinated by the very fact of his or her existence rather than by the information imparted by others will inevitably be accused of arrogance and disrespect. Strong efforts are made to get such children to conform or, at the very least, to refrain from stating their opinions. Expressions of one's own personal reality are usually regarded as irrelevant to the work of the classroom. It is notable that schools which cater for the children of the privileged classes tend to regard their pupils with more individual respect, which is why parents increasingly struggle to send their children to private schools. To passionate advocates of state education like myself, this is a bitter truth to have to swallow, but we must understand that education is at present indissociably bound up with a social structure which values status rather than the human soul. It will take nothing short of a spiritual counter-revolution before this value-system can be changed.

Meanwhile, the idea of the value of one's own life as a constant and marvellous experience does not enter into the way we treat our children. Learning is not concerned with the way things seem to be or with the skills of managing the interpretation of one's own experience. Even our cautious approach to sex education is an exclusively mechanical one. Teachers do not feel themselves able to talk about the real sexual questions of desire and loneliness and love. These things are too real. By the same token, the impulse to put children into school uniform at pubescence has nothing whatever to do with academic standards or an appearance of social equality - it springs directly from a desire to subdue the alarming life-force which becomes so unruly at adolescence, threatening to express itself in its own way instead of in the form of the approved structure.

The connection between the goat and creativity is inescapable. The compliant, sheep-like child who is content to allow its cycle of experience to be filled with the approved names of things rather than the things themselves will accumulate no bursting, inconvenient store of experienced phenomena which demand expression. Sheep children are obedient and useful and approved-of. They achieve accuracy within their range of ability, painstaking if they are not particularly intelligent, academically sound if they are. Within the present system, sheep achieve conspicuous success in high office, for they have an unquestioning respect for the system in which they are engaged. Being disinclined to trust the evidence of direct experience, they seldom encounter any feedback which causes doubt about their own virtue or about the worth of what they are doing. They are narrow and forceful, as effective within a small target area as arrows are. Significantly, their conversation tends to use words expressive of force. They have aims and objectives and speak of aggressive marketing and campaigns and of targeting initiatives. Leading sheep are totally purposeful.

Goats, on the other hand, have an inbuilt suspicion of purpose. A multitude of alternatives are always present in the goat-mind, and total devotion to a single line of thought will always seem restrictive to them. As professional experiencers of life, they will not be attracted by the idea of a steady job with a fixed structure of promotion. They want an element of unexpectedness and even of danger, which is why contemporary society, with its emphasis on safety and close regulation, is increasingly unwilling to accommodate goat-type people, seeing them as "anti-social". Goats are wide-ranging rather than narrow, lateral rather than linear.

At present, we have strong anti-goat (and thus anti-creative) prejudice. At school, the contrast between the two types leads to endless conflict. Very commonly, the teacher is a sheep-type person, for the over-systematisation of teacher training tends to repel and reject goats. A sheep-teacher will find a goat-child thoroughly annoying. Goat children have a lot to say but are not willing to remember anything unless they happen to be interested in it. They are adventurous, impatient and easily bored. They are disobedient and they argue and their work varies from the brilliant to the execrable. They offer glib and often preposterous excuses for their many omissions, and will initiate trouble just for the fun of it. They laugh and fool about and sulk, and fail exams abysmally unless they suddenly decide to work, in which case they can pass them with no great effort. They have no respect for people of importance, and are masters of what the Army calls "dumb insolence". They are an enormous nuisance when young, but they continue to mature and grow throughout their lives because they never stop learning from their direct experience. They are vulnerable to pain although they strive to hide it, and they can eventually become wise. The close-grouping techniques which work well for the controlling of sheep are quite intolerable to goats, and so non-creative discipline simply exacerbates their anarchy.

As far as can be seen, most young children start off with a high degree of goatishness. They all have a strong need to interact with the world which surrounds them, for it is their only way of learning. Early education accepts this, and provides a teaching approach which can use it, but as the years go by, the leaning towards a non-expressive, information-dominated methodology becomes stronger. Pragmatic, down-to-earth intelligence can find little connection with a system calibrated to measure right-or-wrong answers rather than ideas. The examination system favours those with a good memory. It bears no relation at all to the self-testing which creative work imposes, when reference material is freely available but the challenge of what to do with it is laid bare.

To bring children to this one-sided concentration on

memory-training, there must necessarily be a compensatory devaluing of their creative abilities. This process is very visible in secondary schools. Even in a subject as supposedly creative as music, it is possible for a child to pass exams purely through a theoretical knowledge of musical structure and the lives of the composers. Such a study makes no attempt to recognise music as an expression of human feeling. A child's early fingerings of a made-up tune on a piano are, on the contrary, often dismissed with the admonition to "do it properly" from the printed notes of music composed by someone else.

The inability of schools to deal with goat-type children is obvious. Success would result in a mingling of goat and sheep characteristics, with all children finding a comfortable level within a freely-offered range of creative and informational material. At present, the wedge driven between the two types results in alienation of the group which is not catered for. The raising of the school-leaving age has made this alienation more obvious, for it has added a further year of conflict to a process which was already quite irrelevant to the needs of many children. The pupils vote with their feet and with their spray cans (in terms of truancy and vandalism), and yet the lesson is not learned. We seek to blame the child or the abolition of corporal punishment, the teacher, the parents, television, absence of religion, high-rise flats - anything except the educational concept of what a human being really is. Only in conditions of the direst breakdown is the "creative approach" tried, and then it is regarded as therapy rather than education. Reuven Feuerstein, the great Israeli teacher, achieves spectacular success with children written off as ineducable by ordinary schools, using his "enrichment" technique which builds up the child's quality of experience and with it, self-respect and confidence. The truth is, we do not want to give Feuerstein's kind of close attention to an individual child's nature and well-being. The purpose of our education is, as Michael Forsyth pronounced, to produce a skilled work-force. Within such a narrow aim, the problem of the goat must remain an insoluble one.

In a well-balanced society goats are not a problem, but a valued asset. There is a need for their independent common sense. In the goat view, compliance is always a voluntary action, based on consent rather than compulsion; individual judgement is never quite handed over to any greater authority. Societies which suppress their goats are those which fear secretly that their structure could be undermined by dissident opinion. Such fear is a sign that the structure is over-rigid and incapable of healthy elasticity. When pre-war Germany entered into the fanatical inflexibility of Hitler's Fascist dream, the first symptom of the sickness was a deliberate intensification of the sheep characteristics of the population. It was in pursuit of an utterly uniform and consenting flock that people of individual identity were eradicated. Both Jews and Gypsies are almost by definition goats, for the pragmatic, creative intelligence of people who live traditionally without the support of official recognition gives them a self-sufficient skill which the larger society fears and resents. Dictators murder the people they are afraid of. Stalin put down his goats ruthlessly in his determination to suppress articulate intellectual criticism.

All political systems begin as a dream of self-regulating freedom, but as power develops within them, they ossify into rigidity and then dry even further into brittleness, at which point they begin to crack. Democracy decays into authoritarianism. The first stage of this process is a withdrawal of official interest in self-expression among ordinary citizens, for the continuance of the system has become more important than the individual people who constitute it.

We are rapidly approaching this stage. For those who are a successful part of the system, its continuance is desirable, but for many thousands, there is a sense of their profound unimportance in official eyes, coupled with a dispiriting suspicion that a simple political switch will bring no absolute solution. In Scotland particularly, powerlessness is an acute and general discomfort, but there seem to be no recognisable channels through which self-determination can be rediscovered.

The trouble is that the recognisable channels are themselves systematic. It is structuralism itself which has become the danger. An inert public which does not feel itself to be alive and expressive is incapable of self-regulation, and if it is replenished by young people who have been stripped of self-expressive confidence, then the inertia must steadily worsen. Many of the goat-type people who could give society the bounce and lift which it needs are so deprived of constructive outlet for their feelings at school that they turn to other means of expressing them. Creativity has no automatic connection with ethics, so graffiti and vandalism and theft can well become a perverted form of self-expression. William McIlvanney makes this point with perfect accuracy in his story, "The Prisoner", where burglary continues to supply a convict with his only form of imaginative freedom. Creativity is the constructive use of the experience-cycle, and when an approved constructive use is denied, some other outlet must be found.

Our schools are increasingly required to work in an anti-creative way, and the results stare us in the face in the form of depressed and rebellious teenagers who seek nothing except escapism and offer nothing except resentment. Actively and continuously, we turn the creative into the destructive, and we cannot begin to reverse the process until we realise that the goat is indeed necessary.

If we have a degenerate mean environment, the fittest will be the man who is best adapted to degeneracy and meanness; he will survive.

Nietzsche

The Smoke Screen

Creativity is always approved of in principle. Constant lip-service is paid to it in the pronouncements of education authorities and sociologists; it is regarded as a form of human gratification which should be encouraged if possible. If it is not possible, nobody will worry too much, for creativity is too intangible a quality to be greatly missed. Even in individuals, there is often doubt as to whether it really exists - and if it does, there is great difficulty in locating and using it. A smoke screen seems to hang over the whole subject.

An investigation of the nature and history of this smoke screen may help in the task of penetrating it. Early in the life of humankind, creativity was a vital attribute. When people had to live by their own ingenuity without the support of externally-produced heat and light and power, there was a constant need for the imaginative skills which are based on perception and common sense. The building of a boat which would ride safely through stormy water demanded a creative visualisation of the shape best suited to ride the waves. Clothes and kitchen implements, tools and pottery and houses themselves were made as a direct answer to need. Their dynamic quality is lost to us now, for we are taught to think of them as primitive and less good than our modern artefacts. Museums unwittingly reinforce this impression, for a pot taken from its hearth and put in a glass case is shown as a dead thing, an object left behind by progress.

Since progress is now almost exclusively technological, the value we attach to it is also attached to mass production and on the resulting separation of people from an integral, intelligent involvement with their surroundings. A belief that we are in a state of constant improvement brings with it a contempt for all that we have left behind, and this is an unreality which is a large component of the smoke-screen. A more balanced view would perceive that technical progress is accompanied by a regress in hand-skill. There is no gain without loss. The hand-skill was not merely dexterity; it involved an intimate perception of the qualities present in wood and clay, stone and wool. The beauty and subtlety of the things made for common use gave a direct expression to the nature of the person who made them. Any person living today who could make such useful and lovely things without the aid of machinery would command respect for his or her creative ability, and yet such skills were as common as the twentieth-century ability to ride a bike or mend a fuse. Creativity was our background state, which enabled us to survive.

Inevitably, specialisation developed. As techniques became more complex and demanded a workshop rather than an immediate adapting of natural things, professionalism arrived. Millers and smiths and the various wrights sold or bartered their skills, and the idea of earning money came into play, bringing with it a sharper sense of what was useful and what was not. Originally, there was little difference in value between one thing and another, because all things were unique, regardless of whether they were made for holding water or for producing a musical sound, or for the celebration of religious ritual. With the idea of price came a scale of values based on customer demand. A wheelwright or a thatcher could point to the fact that he was earning money, whereas a boy whittling a reed pipe for his own playing could not.

The question of usefulness thickens the smoke-screen considerably, raising the question of creativity's purpose. Now that the every-day artefacts which surround us are made in factories rather than by hand, there seems to be no practical use for creative effort by individual people, and consequently, such effort tends to be regarded as nothing more than a private indulgence. The products of it have no great value unless they are so significant that they can be taken up by the mechanisms of commerce. A book written by an unknown person may be full of wit and wisdom, but in cash terms, it is not valuable because it does not lend itself to mass marketing. The best-selling "block- buster", conversely, must by definition be no more than pleasant, for it must not transcend the process of selling by imposing the nature of its own self too strongly. Anything so distinctive that it can provoke dislike as well as enjoyment is not a thoroughly saleable article. It must be totally inoffensive in order to be universally acceptable.

Creativity, then, is not directly connected to the processes of commerce. If it makes money, it does so by a happy accident rather than by deliberate aim. Clearly, its concern is with some other field - but what is this field, and how do we identify it and, more importantly, justify it?

In trying to answer this question, it is not good enough to adopt the criteria of usefulness and marketability. It may be true that facility in the use of English enables the holder to write a persuasive letter to the Bank, or that attending a pottery class might result in the sale of hand-made ash trays, but this apologia avoids the point. Any serious discussion of creativity has to centre round an acceptance of the human spirit.

In some countries - notably in Russia, despite the ferocious secularism of the recent past - people talk easily and without self-consciousness about the soul. In Britain, the word is overlaid with embarrassment. The adjective "soulful" has degenerated into an expression of sentimentality, more readily applied to a begging Spaniel than a human being. We are curiously unwilling to talk about the centrality of ourselves, the mysterious essence which is identified as the spirit or the soul. We would rather refer to is as the psyche, or even take refuge in the Hindu term of the Atman. Young people will use the trendy phrase, "my karma". There is an evasion of that area of feeling and awareness which is fundamental to every human being and which is expressed through creativity.

The prevailing suggestion is that fundamentality is of no intrinsic worth. It cannot be described accurately or evaluated definitively, so it is not worth considering. Anyone who persists in regarding it as important can be written off as an impractical romantic. Even the churches have fallen victim to this way of thinking. In many cases, ordained members of the clergy have themselves lost conviction that spirituality is the real and central essence of human beings. It is sad to see an attempted "selling" of religion through a consumer-friendly window-dressing of jiving-Jesus pop music and a revamped Bible stripped of poetry.

A defence of creativity must involve a steady and unabashed recognition of the worth of the human spirit. This is becoming an urgent necessity, for our ignoring of it has resulted in terrible dangers. When people are regarded merely as units in some overall plan, the control which they should exercise through the expression of their feelings is over-ruled. Hence, despite world-wide horror in the souls of ordinary people, we approach a total destruction of our natural resources through their rapacious over-selling. The power-structure has ignored the human spirit in pursuit of its own ends.

The mechanics of this successful ignoring must be understood. They are based on the idea that one person can be "better" than another, not in terms of virtuous behaviour, but in terms of intrinsic worth. Seniority is a very well-established value system. Prefects are superior to juniors. Teachers are superior to prefects. The Head is superior to teachers. Above the Head comes a further structure of Governors, Inspectors and the Department of Education. The divisions are rigidly maintained. Is the Queen superior to an unmarried mother living in a squat in south London? Most people would say, yes, she is. Why? One woman is born into circumstances of privilege, another is not - both are possessed of the soul which enables them to look into each other's faces and recognise that here is a human being, nothing more and nothing less.

Self-respect can only begin with an understanding that social and financial structures are artificial things built on top of the bedrock of the common human soul. Creativity is the expression of that soul.

Once this realisation is accepted, a lot of other things become clear. The conventional structure of "success" is revealed to be a very narrow and specific thing, judged only on the basis of skill in certain manipulations; in the management of money and in the selling of work for the maximum return. Reward in terms of a richly fruitful experience is not tangible, so it is not recognised. The young person who goes off with a rucksack to find out what other parts of the world are like is regarded as a "drop-out" who has refused to get on with the proper business of life. Such behaviour is excused as a need to "get it out of his/her system" or, more sympathetically, as a thing which "you can only do when you're young." Living for living's sake cannot be regarded as a serious principle. It is partly for this reason that such strenuous efforts are made to change the ancient way of life pursued by people in "undeveloped" parts of the world. The sight of people going about an unambitious, non-increasing business of working and feeding and playing arouses a deep hostility in those who believe that maximisation of potential is the true purpose of life.

Again and again, we see the pursuit of success held up as the rationale to be respected. Fathers in particular like to boast that a son or daughter is "doing well", though some do not fit this stereotype and will take the more typically female view that "it doesn't matter as long as he/she is happy," though this is often merely an excuse.

In thinking about creativity, one must be clear about the nature of success, disentangling it from the conventional associations of money and acclaim. Success in creative terms is a very real thing, but it can only happen when the mind is fully concentrated on the job in hand. The person who "wins" a musical competition is the candidate who has managed to put the anxiety of the occasion aside, applying every ounce of attention to the detail of his or her performance. The competition is not against the other candidates but against the disorganisation which lurks within the self, ready to interpose nervousness or jealousy of others between the central spirit and the means by which it is seeking to express itself. Similarly, ideas of making money through creative work get in the way of the work itself. Success can never precede creativity as an aim; it can only follow as a result.

To make children strive for success, therefore, is to make them aware that approval of what they do is conditional on their succeeding. It deepens their insecurity and their fear of failure, and many will opt for the "arrived-at" state of self-declared failure rather than continue to dice with the sudden death of its dreaded arrival. Once a child declares, "I can't do that", it is very difficult to rekindle a willingness to try again. Creative teaching must enter into a working partnership over the job in progress, solving the problems of its difficulties in the spirit of doing a tricky crossword together rather than setting a test.

It may be argued that in such basic matters as the teaching of reading, the teacher knows all the answers and the child does not, so a partnership can only be an artificial concept. This is to ignore the child's creative awareness. The purpose of speech is to say something, and the purpose of writing is to write something. The "something" in both cases is within the child's mind, and the teacher's job as a facilitator of the expression of it is a difficult and puzzling one, requiring perceptive skill. Where the spirit of the child is respected as being of equal uniqueness with that of the teacher, the partnership is on a level footing. Because the teacher has a mature store of experience, the flow of energy is from him or her to the children rather than the other way about,but this should not be confused with superiority.

Because creativity is perceived to have different standards from those which govern conventional success, there is a strong impulse among those who direct society to bring creative expression into line with its approved activities. Visual art, for many years regarded as the province of the eccentric and unconventional, has acquired a new respectability, for it can turn out tidy young graduates in Graphics, adept in manipulating the visual image in the service of a sales campaign. The manufacturing of a popular style is big business, for the "image" has long replaced the reality as an object for public consumption. There is a particularly poisonous confusion here, and it has spread its contagion deeply into the body of contemporary art. It is concerned with the prevailing attitude to truth.

All genuine creativity centres round the effort to identify the truth of an experience. This is not to say that truth is the same as realism, for an abstract painting is its own truth; it is a true representation of the ideas which came into the painter's awareness. Increasingly, however, art concerns itself with the lie.

Advertising deals in a hinterland which is so close to the lie that a controlling body has had to be set up to ensure that the statements made or implied are not actually untrue. The aim of advertising is to invest a product with an aura of desirability which is not present in the thing itself. A household cleaner will not radiate speedy efficiency from its position on the supermarket shelf unless it is given a packaging and presentation which suggest these qualities. Whether the product actually merits its description is immaterial. The object of the exercise is not to sell a good cleaner but to sell a cleaner. It only needs to be good enough to avoid gross disappointment - the rest of the qualities are supplied by its "image", created by a designer.

The object of such creation is the establishment of an acceptable half-lie, deliberately constructed in order to influence the buying public. There is no concern with the expression of a personally-realised truth; quite the reverse. The end product is a persuasive illusion, and the artist knows it. In order to feel comfortable about the un-truth of what he or she has produced, all claims to a search for truth must be renounced. Instead, an attitude of light irony must be adopted - a detached, uncommitted willingness to lend strength to any campaign which will pay for an artist's services, as an army pays for mercenary soldiers.

This might be harmless enough when the deception is realised and admitted, but increasingly, the manufactured "image" supplants the reality. In politics, genuine conviction has ceased to be important; the preoccupation is to find a policy which the voters will buy, presented in a form which they find attractive. The shufflings of the Labour party in this area have been deeply self-destructive, for the human spirit yearns for genuineness in a world of commercial illusionism, and to see the simple bluntness of the red flag turned into the simpering winsomeness of a rosebud is to lose faith in the whole democratic process.

Faith has been lost, and rightly. The quasi-creativity of the image-makers works against the expression of the human spirit rather than for it, and there is no point in looking to any institution for deliverance. All structures are the victim of their own structuralism, and of the image in which their makers make them. The only truth in which we may retain belief is in the direct truth of individual experience. It is a shared partaking of reality, just as breathing is a shared partaking of the air, unique to each person, and yet universal.

As the courtiers of the eighteenth century concealed rottenness beneath the powder and periwigs, so our concern with "image" conceals the emptiness beneath it. Only when ordinary people start to rediscover the worth of their own feelings, and undertake the work of expressing those feelings with proper self-respect, can we hope to see any shift towards an exposure of the truth. Until then, the smoke-screen will remain in place.

Why are the streets and squares rapidly emptying,
and why is everyone going back home so lost in thought?

> *Because it is night and the barbarians have not come.*
> *And some men have arrived from the frontiers*
> *and they say that barbarians don't exist any longer.*

And now, what will become of us without barbarians?
They were a kind of solution.

From Waiting For the Barbarians
By C.P. Cavafy.

Scapegoats

Despite all talk of the "enterprise culture", it is expected that enterprise will be used only in the narrow field of profit-making. The apparently irrational and useless creativity of the goat is regarded with deep suspicion, and increasingly, it is made to stand for all that is undesirable. In a profoundly uncreative society, the dissenter can be made to take the blame for any awkward anomalies. Since the prevailing system holds itself to be the ideal one, it cannot accept that it is responsible for both the good and the bad, indissociably linked like the two sides of a coin. The idea of aiming at perfection makes for a fanatical shedding of failure, in an unrealised legacy of Paganism's overthrow.

The ancient system which preceded our perfection-seeking one accepted that life was a good-and-bad mixture, and revered it just the same. We, on the other hand, are taught that life is a worthless mess on which a system must be imposed in order to tidy it up and make it profitable. The more devoutly this system is believed in, the more important it becomes to dissociate it from any responsibility for unpleasantness, and this dissociation can only be achieved through the skilled deployment of scapegoats.

It is significant that the goat lends its name to the function of carrying away blame and so providing an escape from guilt. The goatish association with independence and creativity provides a double justification for this role in a society where conformity is considered the greatest virtue.

The scapegoat system, however, can only work smoothly as long as the chosen goat remains a mythological one, for the object of blame needs to be infinitely flexible. Once the belief in the scapegoat hardens into a specific reality, the fantasy becomes concrete and the situation then becomes one of psychopathic self-delusion. Typical of such rigidities is the opinion expressed to me recently by a young Army officer who had been serving in Northern Ireland.

"This idea that there's a religious conflict in Ireland is rubbish", he said. "And it's nothing to do with being British or not, either. The whole thing is master-minded by one or two 'Mr Bigs'. We'll get them sooner or later, and that will settle it."

There was no dissent from his fellow-officers who were listening. Clearly, the scapegoat personified as "Mr Big" was perfectly real to them, even though they could not be quite sure of his numbers. This belief caused them to feel a hope that every Irishman captured or shot could prove to be Mr Big himself, and so they were able to cherish the idea that they were not an ingredient in the conflict but a lofty, dispassionate means of bringing it to an end.

The situation in Northern Ireland is essentially one of opposed scapegoats. For deep-laid historical reasons, each side believes in the culpability of the other, and has made the opposing faction into a collective scapegoat which can be blamed for all ills. There can be no end to this impasse until the fact of blaming can be identified and internalised by both sides. Once a person thinks, "I do not need to blame anyone for what happened", then he or she is no longer in a state of conflict. For thousands of people trying to lead peaceful lives in Northern Ireland this is already true, but fanaticism robbed of its scapegoat cannot continue, and fighters robbed of their declared enemy are robbed also of their status as fighters, which they cherish. The army, too, is professionally incapable of recognising that blaming is a voluntary activity, so it also enters into the delusion of pursuing a scapegoat, and this leaves scant opportunity for life-respecting common-sense to prevail.

Conflicts are ultimately resolved only when their protagonists become disillusioned (quite literally dis-illusioned) with the mythology which has bound them together. Often, with hindsight, it can be seen that the conflict itself had to happen for the very purpose of revealing the truth behind the mythicality. Thus the Second World War, which most people regard as achieving the *defeat* of fascism was in fact a struggle to expose the untenable nature of the Nazi fantasy to those who had believed in it. The mounting inflammation of the years of battle came to a head as the concentration camps were found and laid open. Only then was it fully understood what a terrible game of scapegoating had underlain the mythology of national superiority.

This understanding may not have been entirely forgotten. Because of it, American soldiers in Vietnam were a little more ready to perceive that they, too, were engaged in an untenable fantasy. Army parlance has it that the troops became *demoralised*, but one might more accurately say that they were *demythologised*. The sense of having stopped pretending is final.

In loosely-organised societies consisting of small groups concerned with the basic processes of living, conflicts with invaders, though sharp, were always eventually resolved with a shrugging acceptance. It made better sense to incorporate the new man-power and new ideas than to continue a mutually destructive struggle. For this reason, Great Britain, as a much-invaded island, has a unique richness of language and of local flavour. Women probably played an important part in this assimilation, for the female attitude is essentially a pragmatic and experiential one, not primarily concerned with matters of status or nationality. Every girl who found herself attracted to a foreign invader for his own personal qualities was making an unwitting statement in favour of real life rather than mythological structures.

The tightly controlled male-dominated societies of today's world believe in their mythologies so literally that they try to present them as hard fact, stripped of mystery. Islam, of course, leans strongly in this direction because it suppresses any female input into its belief-structure, thus laying itself open to a formalism which admits none of the humour and gentleness of common-sense. Ironically, however, our own society has been heavily influenced by a female Prime Minister so dazzled by the masculine virtues that she sought to outdo men at their own game. As a result, we, too, suffer from a rigid structuralism which considers itself to be of prime importance. The system absolves itself from all blame for social violence and distress by the careful establishment of a range of scapegoats which can be deployed to mop up responsibility for any unpleasantness. Thus the unemployed can be made into their own scapegoat by the declaration that "people can get jobs if they want to." A demonstration in which thousands of people take part can be ascribed to the presence of "trouble-makers" and a union-backed strike is interpreted as the efforts of a few unscrupulous leaders to "hold society to ransom". Mr Big is everywhere, a myth as powerful as the Devil himself, ready and willing to perform his scapegoat function, for he is a creation of the system, with no independent reality.

When it is held that the structure is more important than any of its component parts, then it follows that any part which does not fit smoothly into the whole must act as an irritant. Structures are held together by consent. Even in physical terms, it is not overly romantic to see each molecule as a consenting element, for when external stress becomes intolerable, the bonds are broken and the structure disintegrates because the individual molecule can no longer consent to the role in which it was previously cast. In human terms, since the component parts of a social structure consist of conscious elements with a capacity to make decisions, the consent is much more voluntarily given; its withdrawal, however, is equally cataclysmic. For this reason, our current system is, like all systems, acutely sensitive to any signs of unconsent. It can tolerate bad behaviour among the faithful, which is why drunken bank clerks on cross-Channel ferries are tutted over but not hated. Conversely, the Druidic followers who try to go to Stonehenge for the summer solstice are very deeply hated. The extraordinary fury unleashed on such people indicates a subconscious fear of what they represent, for although their withdrawal of consent to the system may seem puny, it is clearly expressed, and so it must not go unpunished.

In the official mind, there remains a whiff of heresy about people who do not subscribe to the rule of money and convention. Their evident pursuit of life for life's sake is a reminder of the pre-Christian life-worship which still remains anathema to those in authority, and it continues to arouse instincts of the witch-hunt. Travelling people incur rigid intolerance, for people who place no reliance on the much-vaunted "security" of property ownership are suspected to draw their evident confidence from some other, unknown source. Here, too, there is a connection with the Paganism which continues to encapsulate all that is most hated by those who direct our society, and this explains the traditional association of Gypsies with powers of prophecy and "the evil eye". Their independence remains a kind of power, for, being without tangible privilege of any kind, they cannot be threatened with its withdrawal. They are outside the "stick-and-carrot" process which keeps most people tied to a job and mortgage repayments.

Independence is respected in the rich who can claim to have bought a right to it, but it is hated in the poor. People who are voluntarily poor are considered at best to be deeply eccentric, even if they are credited with the saintliness of Mother Teresa, and where their non-conformity lacks her self-evident meekness, it is deeply suspect. The poor have an important part to play in a capitalist society, for they should demonstrate through their subservience and acceptance of failure that a "sink" of misery awaits all those who do not strive to succeed in conventional terms. Hence, there is a particular loathing of socially insignificant youngsters who demonstrate their independence and cockiness through riding motor bikes and wearing calculatedly offensive clothes.

The official intolerance of all these dissenting groups expresses an element of fear. Again, this may be a subconscious throw-back to the more radical fear of life itself, the ancient force which Christianity seeks to tame and harness. The horror of Goddess-worship centres on the human sacrifice which once formed part of its ritual, and it may have been this which underlay the widespread belief in the last century that Gypsies stole children away. It is ironic to reflect on the newspaper reports of children who really are stolen away, not by gypsies, but for sacrifice in the worship of money, their suffering recorded on videotape for highly profitable sale to those of sick mind. Just as the abhorrence of human sacrifice fuelled the overthrow of the Goddess religion, so an abhorrence of the unscrupulous making of money begins to form a counter-movement which may one day reinstate the importance of human feeling.

Meanwhile, the prevailing system accurately identifies its enemies as those who do not share its belief in the values of getting and spending. Chief among these enemies are teachers. They are subjected to a subtle and continual campaign of discredit, not because they are inefficient - that is the mythological scapegoat - but, on the contrary, because they are efficient, at their best (or worst, in the official view), in their efforts to enable children to think for themselves. Good teaching, by its very nature, develops the child's ability to value its own unique being. The achievement of a creative teacher is the positive encouragement of independence and creativity in his or her pupils, and this is profoundly counter to the overall intention of our present administration. Our teachers are badly paid and of little socially-recognised value, and these things are no accident. Writing in 1990, it would be naive to accuse the Government of folly - this is not the case. It is a well-informed and sharply intelligent body, and its education policy is consciously shaped towards the production of a compliant work-force which is skilled in the abilities needed for the making of money both for the workers themselves and for the individual or institution employing them.

Primary school teachers do not see themselves as directly ruled by this labour-market aspect of education, and they deal more fundamentally with the creative nature of the child. Because there is an inverse relationship between creativity and perceived value, the conventional view is that education becomes more serious and important as the age of the child increases. In the secondary school, the upper end of which connects directly to the job market, the attitude of most teachers turns away from creativity. Many of them seek to justify the educational process in purely commercial terms, promising that diligence will lead to the reward of profitable employment. For many children, this is palpably untrue, and they know it, and since they are offered no other philosophical view of education's purpose, they cannot see that any logical rationale lies behind what they are asked to do. To them, it often appears to be no more than discipline for discipline's sake, a set of arbitrary demands which are both boring and vindictive, designed to expose and ridicule their incapacity. School becomes a battle between "us and them" which is never quite resolved. Leaving full-time education may bring the immediate conflict to an end, but the continuing hostility often runs on from generation to generation as children inherit the resentment and truculence which parents continue to feel about their own school experience.

Such children are conventionally regarded as the failures of the education system, but in fact they unwittingly play a useful role in the current structure of society; they become scapegoats. The process of edging them towards this position starts while they are still at school, where their disruptiveness is regarded as a crime against the school body rather than a symptom of acute discomfort in the child. The school can thus preserve the illusion that everything would be fine were it not for the presence of these trouble-makers. This prevents teachers from taking a clear view of how the system relates to the child, substituting a simplistic desire to get rid of the fifteen-year-old Mr Big who is upsetting everything.

The school's vigorous defence of itself masquerades as a discipline which is for the good of all, but in fact it is usually nothing more than a counter-attack on individual offenders, and this merely establishes their status more firmly. Any reproof or punishment carried out in front of other children is in particular a formalisation of the child as sinner and as victim. It is a dangerous game, for the class may well see the attacked child as victim rather than sinner, and the resultant polarization will be against the teacher.

By the time a child leaves school, it will be clear both to the teachers and to the pupil whether he or she is a co-operator with the system or not. This is a distinction which approximates roughly to the "sheep and goats" categorisation, and it plays a major part in determining the pattern of the child's future life. It is not the school's job to change the category to which a child belongs, and at present much time and energy is wasted in an effort to do this. A respect for the creative self-determination which is latent in every human being would enable us to stop the production of failures who are blamed for their own failure.

It is vital for teachers to be aware of the lasting effects of what they say and do. The actual content of lessons is almost immaterial compared with the importance of the teacher's attitude to the children and to the way in which they are able to work. If we stop producing scapegoats, then we may be able to look steadily at the real implications of the situation in which our society is involved.

A Mexican potter was selling beautifully decorated plates, no two of which were alike.

"How much are these?" a tourist enquired.

"Ten pesos each, senor."

"I would like a set of six identical plates. How much would that be?"

"For six of the same design? Eighty pesos, senor."

"But that is more than six times ten! I am giving you a bulk order, so you should do it for less money, not more."

"No, senor. If I have to make six plates all the same, you must pay me for the boredom."

From a story told by Raimundo Pannikar

Boredom

As a child, I thought I would remember for ever how bored I was. Looking back, the memory of having had this thought remains clear, though the sharpness of the discomfort itself has faded, as all pains do. But to ask of a class of children, "Has anyone ever been bored?" is to have every hand in the room up. Boredom is a universal experience.

Usually, boredom is regarded as a negative thing, as if the person suffering from it has relapsed into a childish desire to be amused. With maturity, we are supposed to be busy and interested in whatever it is we have to do. Anyone who admits to being bored is declaring a disinterest which can seem like superiority - a dissatisfaction with circumstances, a failure to buckle down to the inevitably tedious business of living.

I was given a different view of it by an old friend, "Gelignite Jim", who had spent most of his life blowing tree-stumps out of the ground with dynamite. After suffering a stroke, he retreated into the quiet life. I asked him if he felt bored. "No", he said. "Only when people come and talk to me." It was not a rebuff - simply a statement of fact. With a life-time's accumulation of experience stored in his mind, he found it interesting to muse and remember, and the presence of a chattering visitor acted as a block to this process.

The idea of boredom as a positive and uncomfortable imposition will have a ring of familiarity to the many children who suffer from it. There is a sense of being prevented from doing something less approved-of but more interesting, and so the imposed circumstances are described as "boring". For young children, a more generalised boredom takes the form of irritable discontent and a feeling that nothing is interesting. In either case, interest is the missing factor, and lack of it is felt as a deprivation, just as lack of food is felt as hunger.

This sensation is, in experiential terms, a perfectly true one. Thinking again of the "bulb" diagram of creative functioning, it is obvious that an impediment lodged in the processing of experience is almost literally "a spanner in the works". Its presence will have certain effects. (Illustration 18 on following page)

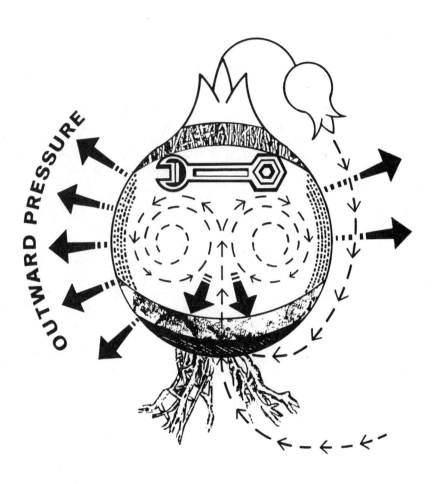

OUTWARD PRESSURE

Illustration 18

87

Let us suppose that the organism shown here represents a child in a classroom, presented with a subject of study in which he or she can find no interest. Leaving aside any question of how the situation has arisen or what should be done about it, one can take a purely mechanical view of what is happening within the child's being.

The experiences entering into the awareness via the senses are partly from an external source and partly of the child's own making. The external ones will consist of the classroom, the physical sense of sitting at a desk and being aware of the other children and of what is happening outside the room, and, most of all, the lesson. If the lesson has not been understood, the experience of it cannot pass through the reasoning process and emerge as the specific activity of the appropriate work. Instead, it lodges at the junction of feeling and reason and makes a blockage. The inward movement of experience does not stop, and is added to by the child's own feelings of frustration and of imagined and infinitely preferable circumstances. This "short circuit" rapidly adds to the build-up of pressure within the feeling-area. Blocked by the impossibility of finding expression, it turns back and can find no escape.

The mounting pressure squeezes against its surroundings, causing discomfort to the self. Emotion is pushed upward along the outer edges of the being, and reason, separated from feeling by the blockage and deprived of material on which it can work, thins and becomes irrelevant to what is happening. As a result, no constructive action can take place, and the specific activity which the child is expected to produce withers into negation.

To the outside observer, a child in this state will be fidgety and irritable, disinclined to get on with the set work but constantly trying to introduce some other activity of an illicit sort. Scolding produces sulking and a renewed effort to disrupt the proceedings, and the situation becomes more and more difficult to control.

If, at this point, the teacher can take a new initiative with the child, expressing the point of the lesson in a different way so that understanding is achieved, the blockage may break up and a normal throughput of experience (including the lesson itself) may be resumed. The longer the blockage is left in place, the more solid and well-established it becomes. For this reason, there are many children in the upper forms of secondary schools who are in a state of fixed and permanent boredom, convinced that anything a teacher says can only add to it.

Superficially, it may look at this point as if there is no valid comparison between boredom and physical hunger, since, on the contrary, the "bulb" appears to be bursting with unused experience. This would be true if the organism was a static thing, but it is in fact a process rather than an object, and the state of its well-being is related entirely to the free flow of its energies. It is very much like the digestive system. If this is blocked by the ingestion of a foreign object or by the presence of a pathogen such as a growth, the effect on the body will be a deprivation of nutrition which no amount of additional food will cure. The same deprivation will of course take place if there is simply not enough food, and this is also true of the creative cycle.

Here again, there will be a build-up of pressure because of the mounting emotion generated by the situation. It finds an outlet in the illicit activities familiar to anyone who has been bored; doodling, day-dreaming, conducting of conversations with others either by written note, facial expressions or whispers, secret perusal of other reading matter and interjection of irrelevant remarks. And all this can happen within a situation where the teacher is still in control of the class. Where such control has been lost, the way is open to far more rampant substitute activity such as full-scale eating and drinking and the playing of board-rubber football. Unpleasant though this is for those in charge, it at least represents a form of continuing activity, like a loud warning signal. It is an outburst. Much more dangerous for the child is the inburst which results from the effect of boredom at the opposite extreme.

Where there is absolutely no input into the experiential cycle at all, there will eventually be a drop in the internal pressure of the organism. For a while, it may be sustained by its own production of emotion, but in most people this will give way to an admission of inadequacy and depression. They are suffering at this point from a total starvation of experiential fuel. The obvious example of a situation of this kind is imprisonment. As Jimmy Boyle points out in his book, "A Sense of Freedom", a secure unit is constructed for maximum boredom. It is totally bare, devoid of anything which can be moved or used in any way. This is not accidental - it is designed to "break the spirit" and cause the prisoner to admit his inferiority and his absolute dependence on the system. To achieve this, the last traces of self-respect must be erased. It takes a person of exceptional inner resources to withstand this treatment. More normally, some kind of reduction of the self is achieved.

Here, the whole functioning has been reduced to a minimal tick- over which, from the authorities' point of view, is the desired state. The prisoner has an almost unfeeling acceptance of the situation and does not think of expressing emotion through any untoward activity. The cutting-off of experiential input has resulted in a drop in active feeling, and this can be seen as a drop in pressure. In order to accommodate this changed state, and the approaching near-vacuum which it threatens, the whole organism must shrink, just as the tissues of a plant will do when they are deprived of water. A prisoner with a leathery flexibility of the self will be able to adapt to this deprivation as a cactus can, but for more vulnerable organisms, the picture is very different.

When a young person is taken into custody, the cutting-off of accustomed experience is traumatic. Even the most brash of self-declared young villains will find the barren-ness of the situation surprisingly painful, and for those who are not brash at all but merely confused or inadequate, a condition of crisis is set up.

An organism which is used to being fed by a richness of supportive and familiar experience is suddenly deprived of it. The resulting drop in internal pressure is dramatic. The sense of boredom is acutely painful, and the self-awareness of most young people is not tough enough to adapt quickly to changed circumstances; it is only the muscular, cynical self of a person who has long given up expecting any support which is able to accomplish the drastic changes involved in arrest and imprisonment. For the inexperienced boy or girl, the only knowledge is of what he or she has previously been, and there is a desperate need to cling to that sense of identity. This means that the dimensions of the self are not flexible, but try to maintain their previous shape, in a fragile rigidity which is as vulnerable as a light bulb. As the drive towards a state of internal vacuum approaches, the only awareness will be of the inadequacy of the self to withstand it. That single awareness will barge straight through the intelligence of feeling into the reason, which has no alternative but to interpret it as a need to end the unbearable circumstances. With inexorable logic, the correct response to the signal will be to pass it through into appropriate action, which can only be self-destruction. Every remaining scrap of experience and feeling blossoms in the one specific activity which is still available.

The achievement is an arid one, resulting in the impersonal immortality of a statistic and the anguish of all those who knew the victim and who wonder endlessly about the nature of the distress which caused the self-destruction.

The statistics themselves are revealing. According to the Home Office, thirty-two men (no women) killed themselves while in custody during the year 1988-89. During the same year, a total of 2,025 detainees injured themselves, 368 of them "with apparent suicidal intent". Inquests on a further ten deaths were awaited. This gives a suicide rate per 100,000 which, even discounting these ten, runs at roughly twice the British rate of 17.6. (W.H.O.) A study by Dr Enda Dooley, consultant psychiatrist at Broadmoor special hospital, of 296 suicides in England and Wales found that the biggest group, 40 per cent, were those who could not cope with being in prison. The report adds, "The suicide rate was proportionately much higher among prisoners on remand than those sentenced."

Remand prisoners constitute a group which will contain people other than "old lags". There will also be the young and inexperienced, the frightened and the insecure. A regime which deliberately removes any element of interest from the surroundings in which these people are kept must recognise that it acts to intensify the inadequacy which is already present. Measures to prevent suicide attempts by increasing supervision do not make any move towards understanding the problem. To be healthy in social terms as well as psychological ones, a human being must be in a state of active experience-using.

Boredom is symptomatic of an interruption to this process, either through deprivation of raw material or a blockage of its throughput, and we should take it more seriously than we do. It gives rise to pain, and it can be fatal, for it gradually erodes the idea that life can be interesting enough to be worth living. Boredom sets up such an imperative inner demand for experience that other considerations pall. The experience supplied by the use of drugs, for instance, is a respite from boredom, and the knowledge that it will in the long term have terrible effects only adds to the sense of stepping away from unbearable tedium.

Where no value can be found in the ordinary state of living, there can be no real inducement to give up the much more pleasant experience brought about by the use of hallucinogens, and this is something which must be understood. Attacks on "drug abuse" are unlikely to be effective unless the real reasons for its attractiveness are recognised.

We seek to suppress the symptoms of boredom, much as we tell a child with a cold to wipe its nose. Stoicism is a strong element in the British, and we admire uncomplaining endurance. A friend of mine was dismayed recently to hear an educational psychologist tell a child, "Growing up means we have to do lots of things we don't want to do." This picture of adult life as a state of permanent endurance is often imparted to children, with an air of gloomy triumph. "Just you wait until you're my age - you'll know what it's like then."

At one time, endurance was a valuable quality, essential for the survival of cold winters and times of privation. For many people, it is still needed in the daily battle against insufficient resources - but there has been a subtle shift of emphasis. There is no longer any element of triumph. Subsistence agriculture is a remorselessly hard way of life, full of cruelties and disappointments, and yet these difficulties are balanced by the satisfaction of bringing into the house the grain and vegetables of one's own growing. Where endurance of hardship results in the continuance and even the enjoyment of life, then it can be undertaken in the spirit of challenge. But where it is simply a prerequisite, with no visible effect on living circumstances, there is no challenge and no triumph. Instead, an unthinking respect for endurance has taken the place of any dynamism. It is not so much endurance as acceptance, and it demands no strength, but rather a voluntarily-undertaken weakness. "Putting up with it" requires a shrug rather than a gritting of the teeth, but we have not perceived the difference, and so acceptance is thought to be as virtuous as endurance once was.

The misunderstanding is a profound one, and boredom is a symptom which can tell us a lot about the malaise which has assailed us. Boredom is caused by a natural demand for active, first-hand experience, so it is not assuaged by supplying second-hand information and advice. As all parents lament, the younger generation does not learn from the experience of mothers and fathers, but insists on finding out for itself, often at the cost of much suffering. The young have no instinct to protect themselves from painful experience; only to protect themselves from second-hand experience, which is of a totally different order and is obviously intrinsically unsatisfactory. They fantasize about adventures wherein they can triumph over opposition and win admiration and gratitude by their daring - hence the popularity of the "Dungeons and Dragons" cult, and the common conviction among young males that toughness is an essential attribute.

All this shows that the need to encounter real experience is very fundamental, and the young are still aware of it. In the days when all people were directly concerned with their own physical survival, the young simply took their place in this struggle, but in contemporary life (particularly in the city) the struggle lacks tangible reality. There is no triumph to be found in surviving for one more week on Supplementary Benefit or in completing another five days in a tedious job. Coping with these circumstances demands a skill of sorts, but there is a curious sense of unimportance about it, as if this is not the central business of life at all, but a prolonged and irritating interruption of it. The same feeling of superimposition must have attended such things as the annual visit of the factor to an isolated community for the collection of the toll considered due for the privilege of living there. To hand over a bale of tweed or an animal in recognition of the payment must have seemed a harsh irrelevance. The photographs of St. Kildans, for instance, taken on such occasions, show faces which have set aside their customary determination; the marks of it are there in the strength and cragginess, but it is overlaid with a cautious uncertainty. The arrival of the man from the mainland is extraneous to the real business of life. His effect on them is a superimposition of his reality on theirs, a temporary interruption. He causes acute discomfort.

It is not difficult to see the world of the factor enlarged to become a city estate in which people live, paying rent for the privilege just as the St. Kildans did. But, for the "scheme" dweller, the factor's visit never ends and there is no return to the reality in which work is directly related to survival. Life is permanently encompassed by a concept which originated elsewhere, in the minds of planners or the businessmen who developed a housing enterprise. The experience of it is essentially second-hand rather than first-hand.

The distinction may seem to be an over-fine one; after all, awareness is awareness, regardless of what phenomena enter the consciousness. Is not the act of experiencing, according to the model I suggest, more important than the nature of what is experienced? Surely it is all "grist to the mill"?

The answer, it seems to me, is that the act of experiencing is the fundamental condition of human existence, so it must be regarded as of prime importance. Precisely *because* it is so important, the selection of phenomena to be experienced is equally critical. The distinction is virtually the same as that between raw and cooked food. Raw food (or raw experience) is the stuff itself, unchanged by any human intervention. Cooked food, on the other hand, has been subjected to the creative functioning of another person. The result may be wonderful, just as architecture may be, but it is still someone else's construct. The categories define themselves very easily. First-hand experiences are interactions with the natural state, in its broadest sense. Water and the sky, earth and the things which grow from it are all completely first-hand. Direct contact with animals and birds of the wild kind, with the weather and with landscape, owes nothing to the influence of other people. We seek the same reality of contact in human relationships as well, but often meet only the established conventions of behaviour, which are from the realm of the second-hand. This category includes all human-made things, from the products of art down to the multiple, all-enclosing surfaces of the city. Television is second-hand, for it presents a pre-formed image. Much of education is second-hand.

Within each of these categories, there is a range of potential experiences from the sublime to the appalling. First-hand experience can produce moments of acute self-realisation but it also has danger and horror. It encompasses birth and death, growing and sickness, and the loneliness of knowing that one lives. Second-hand experience exists in a narrower compass, because it is limited to the products of humans, but it covers the magical excitement of another mind's imaginings given permanence as music or the soaring grandeur of a cathedral as well as the meanness of housing estates.

There are close overlaps which make it seem as if the categories are intermixed. One man may kill another in a back street, but the death is a first-hand happening in a second-hand setting - which is why there is such a pungency about the juxtaposition of the two elements in writing and film-making. Listening to a radio play can produce a sense of direct experience which is partially true because, lacking a visual input, the listener is free to construct one. The less complete the illusion is, the more personal the statement can be. A sketch on the back of an envelope retains the first-hand nature of its own surface and of the movement of the hand and the pencil which made the marks on it, but a naturalistic oil painting of perfectly meticulous finish attempts to sink itself into the illusion it seeks to create - namely, that the viewer is seeing the reality which the artist saw. A roomful of such paintings will usually be dismissed by the young as "boring".

Boredom, then, is not only a symptom of the need for experience; it is a need for direct, first-hand experience. We see this need expressed in an endless variety of ways. Advertisements for holidays stress the "unspoilt" quality of their beaches and cottages, and some make a deliberate point of their rawness and wildness, offering Himalayan trekking or Arctic adventure. People retreat to their weekend cottages and return with a certain air of superiority after grappling with a recalcitrant Aga or clearing the water supply of the pine needles which have clogged the filter after heavy rain.

Young people are more easily bored than anyone else, as they are in the process of laying down stores of usable experience for later reference. It is precisely because these stores are incomplete that youngsters cannot identify the cause of their boredom. They do not question that their surroundings have been designed and provided by other human beings or that all their experience is supplied in a second-hand way. Activities are usually directed towards the acquiring of money followed by the spending of it, and teenagers grope within this process for the means of transcending boredom. Bright clothes and loud music serve the purpose to some extent, but there is still a sense that life is not exciting. The first-hand reality of risk offers a great attraction here, for they sense that "raw" experience stops at nothing, and can give them a reality of event which the approved-of provisions cannot touch.

It is this thirst for direct experience which leads to much of the behaviour which we regard as undesirable. The intensely participatory but ritualised violence of the football supporters' Saturday afternoons incorporates a sense of gutsy reality which touches ancient instincts. Dismaying though it is, the impulse to smash the second-hand environment which surrounds these young men on their way back to the television and their second-hand homes is a powerful statement couched in terms as crude as a scream.

The same overwhelming need for strong primary experience underlies the use of drugs. The reason why addiction is so difficult to treat is that nobody can offer a counter-attraction of equal value. It is significant that people with a good income and an interesting life can support a heroin habit which does not become overwhelming - there are far more "self-contained" addicts of this kind than is generally recognised. In such cases, there is a balance of attractive realities which keeps the use of hallucinogens in a minor place. For people lacking even the basic human recognition which existence should bring, emergence from heroin's happy dream is intolerable.

It would be naive to suppose that "creative" activities can act as an easy substitute in such cases of pathological breakdown of self-respect. Sculpture classes and a poet in residence cannot be applied like sticking plasters to such severely destroyed organisms. We must look further back to the formulating influences of which we are hardly aware.

The tangible presence of poverty is a necessity in the current structure of our society, for it provides the stick in the "stick-and-carrot" system which drives it on. One need only look quite superficially at the buildings which house schools to see how blatantly the favours are bestowed or denied. The conventions are well-established; cedar trees and lawns, towers, porticos, gravelled drives - what school is this? If a television camera pans across such a setting, the viewers know at once that the children of wealthy parents are educated here. The treeless yards and breeze-block walls of the average state secondary school make an equally clear announcement. No more expenditure can be afforded. Children of ordinary families are educated in these buildings, and the cost of the job has been fixed at a low level. Parents who want something better are free to go out and buy it if they can. Let them eat cake.

Here again, the question of boredom presents itself. There is an intense, almost aggressive monotony inherent in the architecture of cost-controlled buildings. The repeated units of windows and wall-spaces admit no variation - their visual rhythm is remorseless, a regular thump like hammer-blows. The same is true of municipal housing, with its utter regularity of repeated rectangles. Even the least educated human eye has an acute recognition of the fact that an old cottage, hand-built by someone a long time ago for the direct purpose of providing shelter and warmth and for the sense of being in one's chosen place, has a beauty which is notably absent in mass-supplied housing. The building of such a cottage is a direct personal experience, a first-hand reality, full of the essential interest which made its construction necessary. The same is true of the great cathedrals, put together over centuries from the direct need to express a love of God. Personal feeling is deeply inherent in such structures. The village school used at one time to look rather like a small church with its pitched roof and pointed porch and belfry. Such a building implied that what went on inside it was lofty and serious, like religion itself, but its small scale brought it down to domestic proportions and made it clear that this was a junior process, not yet attaining full grandeur.

Undoubtedly, old school buildings were dark and insanitary,and lessons were conducted within them which were often dull, enforced by methods which verged on the sadistic, but, good or bad, they were never impersonal. They were charged with a Biblical vision of attainable goodness and were prepared to use physical assault in pursuit of it. They could inspire horror or triumph, but they could not be ignored. Their power lay in an absolute recognition that each child had a spirit to be wrestled for.

Uneasiness about the Christian domination of education set in after the Second World War, when Britain began to become more obviously a multi-racial society and the government of the day held the agnostic views which traditionally went with socialism. The secularisation of education went ahead rapidly, with a replacement of dark, chapel-windowed schools by modern buildings in glass and concrete. At the time, it was exciting, and the new humanism seemed to offer an opening-up of possibilities from which every child in the country could benefit. Ideas flourished, some of them good and some crazy, and money was spent generously on educational provision. There was a heady sense of boundless potential, and this should not be forgotten when we deride the glass palaces of the post-war period. The religious neutrality of both the buildings and the educational outlook were given a spiritual content then by a passionate belief that the ordinary child mattered in its own right. We had fought a war which, we thought, would stand for all time as a sign that the individual was too precious a thing to be subjected to any regime which regarded it as a disposable unit. Democracy was the tangible reality for which so many people had died, and their potential children with them.

It was a short-lived ideal. By the seventies, economic recession had arrived as a permanent dread which was to hang like a ghost over the grave-yard of humanism. The priorities shifted, and the management of insufficient funds settled in as the first duty of local authorities.

The effect on schools was disastrous, not so much for the cuts in spending as for the changed attitude which underlay them. Education could not retrieve the lost Christian morality which had been swept away with the oak-edged slates and fixed benches of the pre-war schools. Its new scrupulousness in refraining from indoctrination had dove-tailed perfectly with the fervent belief in human worth which had held sway in the fifties and sixties, but human worth began to be a less valuable quality in the seventies. The relaxed individualism which had given rise to the hippie movement decayed into an indifference to everyone except the self, and it began to seem naive to profess a real concern for the disadvantaged.

Against this opportunistic background of self-help, enthusiastically supported by a Conservative government, schools found themselves without a tenable spiritual attitude. Ironically, Christianity had put itself even further out of official favour with the involvement of many devout Christians in the peace and anti-nuclear movements, so the Church was no longer seen by the authorities as an unquestionable upholder of approved views. Except in specifically denominational schools, its influence continued to wane - but the waning of humanism, which had hardly had time to be recognised as a guiding philosophy, happened even faster.

The twin voids have never been filled. Humanism tipped over with fatal easiness into human self-indulgence, where it remains firmly ensconced. Christianity, with its God conceived to be outside and separate from the human condition, increasingly fails to make contact with life as most people experience it, particularly as the Christian uneasiness about worldly wealth sets up an important point of difference from the prevailing ethic.

It is this moral and spiritual emptiness which is so unerringly reflected in the very appearance of most of our schools today. Teachers do their very best to disguise it, with children's work mounted on gaily-coloured paper covering the walls, but the buildings themselves convey contempt for those who use them. One cannot imagine a Bank where buckets are placed to catch the rainwater which drips through ceilings - or, indeed, one where the walls consist of painted breeze block. Symbolism is very often accidental, but its language is universally understood. The visually boring school is designed to bore, because the acceptance of boredom is the fundamental lesson which underlies all others. In a society which works exclusively on the idea of success or failure, a large number of people must be brought at an early age to accept uncomplainingly that they are failures, for they act as a stable bottom-line against which success can be perceived and measured.

The sense of boredom is, as we have seen, a natural response to experiential deprivation, and it should be regarded as a valuable diagnostic pointer. In an experiment at Drummond High School, Edinburgh, when children were asked for their opinion on the curricular content of future lessons, they were "surprisingly conservative" in their choice, as the Depute Head put it. They opted for the basic skills, and offered a trade of good behaviour for a promise "not to nag". The underlying purpose of the scheme was to introduce a more creative and self-determining element into the children's school experience, and it quickly began to pay dividends in terms of reduced friction and a better working atmosphere. Boredom was tackled, not by attacking the sufferer for being bored, but by treating the cause of the affliction.

This shift in approach may seem to be slight, but it represents a move which may lead to a new spiritual justification for education, consisting of a respect for the human spirit and an offering of readiness to trust in it. On such terms, a working partnership between teacher and taught, employer and employed, can be established and developed. It runs counter to the mindless respect for the ruling structures which is at present demanded, but all good teachers have used it for years. Without the self-respect which is a recognition that one's own use of experience is uniquely valuable, there can be no development. For some, there cannot even be continuance.

Untitled Poem

He wanted to explain things, but no-one cared,
So he drew.
Sometimes he would just draw and it wasn't anything
He wanted to carve it in stone or write it in the sky.
He would lie out on the grass and look up at the sky, it would
    only be the sky and the things inside him which needed
    saying.
And it was after that he drew the picture.
It was a beautiful picture. He kept it under his pillow and
    would let no-one see it.
And he would look at it every night and think about it.
And when it was dark and his eyes were closed he could see it
    still.

And it was all of him and he loved it.
When he started school he brought it with him
Not to show anyone, but just to have it with him like a friend.
It was funny about school.
He sat in a square brown desk like all the other square brown
　　desks and he thought it would be red. And his room was a
　　square brown room, like all the other rooms.
And it was tight and close. And stiff.
He hated to hold the pencil of chalk, with his arms stiff and
　　his feet flat on the floor, stiff, with the teacher
Watching and watching.
The teacher came and spoke to him.
She told him to wear a tie like all the other boys.
He said he didn't like them and she said it didn't matter.
After that they drew. And he drew all yellow and it was the way
　　he felt about morning.
And it was beautiful.
The teacher came and smiled at him. "What's that?" she said.
"Why don't you draw something like Ken's drawing?
Isn't it beautiful?"
After that his mother bought him a tie and he always drew aero-
　　planes and rocket ships like everyone else.
And he threw the old picture away.
And when he lay out alone looking at the sky it was big and
　　blue and all of everything that he wasn't anymore.
Anymore.
He was square and brown inside and his hands were stiff.
And he was like everyone else, all the things inside him that
　　needed saying didn't need it anymore.
It has stopped pushing. It was crushed stiff.
Like everything else.

The sudden use of the present tense in the penultimate line betrays the state of the writer, a fourteen-year-old boy, whose cycle of experience-using has been brought to a halt. Shortly afterwards, he committed suicide.

"Teach the child what principles govern our emotions and the physiology of the many and diverse stirrings within us. For it seems to me that the first lessons with which we should irrigate the child's mind should be those which teach him to know himself."

Michel de Montaigue 16th century French philosopher

Discipline

There is a strong tendency in the public mind to associate creative people with indiscipline. It is an idea which is hugged to the chest almost defensively, as an excuse for claiming that creativity is an elusive and difficult business, too anarchic for ordinary people to cope with. Wildness and eccentricity are held to be inevitable attributes of "artistic" people, who are felt to belong in a category of talented oddness which separates them from normal human beings. Within this different and Bohemian world, it is assumed that artists drift about in an enjoyable state of irresponsibility, waiting for inspiration to arrive and cause them to do something remarkable, with virtually no real effort.

This is, of course, a myth, but it is one which is constantly reinforced. Creative people themselves develop a disregard for the restrictions imposed by convention, and this is a necessary discarding, for it frees the mind to consider all possibilities. It is, however, an internal process in which anyone can share; creativity exists in all people, no matter how unremarkable in appearance and behaviour. The late William Coldstream, who was Professor of Fine Art at the Slade School, was as dry and dark-suited as a solicitor's clerk and Henry Moore might have passed for a bricklayer's mate - wild appearance is much more characteristic of those who want to *appear* to be artistic. Art students often make an art of themselves, with expressive enthusiasm spilling out into the colour and shape of their clothes and hair, make-up and ornament. It is amateur actors who will "emote" loudly about their interpretation of a role; professionals get on with the job.

Decorative living is in itself creative to some extent, but this does not disguise the fact that nobody can be creative without working at it. Even the buying of clothes (generally regarded as a recreational affair) can involve creative effort. Colours must be evaluated, cut and shape carefully considered, garments tried on and scrutinised in the changing room mirror. Incoming experience is being sifted by an active feeling-intelligence, and there will be no blossoming into the specific activity of purchase until the best use of that experience has been decided on.

The fact that this may be enjoyable does not put the activity into a non-work category. We are conditioned to think that work must be unpleasant and compulsory, so we assume that voluntary effort which brings its own reward cannot be work. This attitude has come about because the majority of people are deprived of the satisfaction of creative work, so they have to make a virtue of the suffering imposed on them by their dull or over-demanding jobs. The virtue is essential, otherwise there is no access to self-respect, and no real justification for continuing to live.

This inverted value-system results in a deep suspicion of enjoyment. Even when people like what they do, they often protest that it is tiring and difficult and under-paid, as if to assure the enquirer that they are of the worthy mass of work-endurers. Not to be of the mass is to risk being thought odd and pretentious, possessed of a talent or cleverness which precludes membership of the good majority. This is one of the most fundamental elements in the British class system, far more permanent and deep-rooted than wealth. The structure-dominated attitude which holds that work is something to be traded for money reaches far into the most powerful ranks of our society, bringing into high office an outlook which used to be thought "working class". Frugality, respect for one's betters and an assumption that culture is an intellectual self-indulgence remain admired qualities. "Knowing one's place" is an essential attribute for those who must work their way up through a promotion system, for without humbleness and striving, there can be no triumph in achieving seniority.

Thus, the cheerful piracy of the free-booting nineteenth-century industrialists, although nominally admired, has been converted into a tightly-organised structure of self-interest. The difference is the equivalent of Long John Silver joining the Mafia. Individual roguery is systematised into a distasteful and rigid hierarchy of extortion, which is inexorable and ultimately boring, because the idea that self-expressive enterprise can flourish within it is largely a false one. In practical terms, as thousands of people have found out, to move from employment to self-employment, or from self-employment to the employing of others involves entanglement with officially-imposed regulations of great complexity. The organic expansion from market stall to Marks and Spencer which remains the entrepreneurial dream is, nowadays, no more than a dream. The reality is that one must enter the structure.

This structure is in itself a political element. It transcends the class divisions, which began to crumble, ironically, during the Labour administration, the benevolence of which made it possible for working class people to cast off the shackles which belonging to that category had previously imposed. The traditional basis of politics began to break up at that point, though politicians themselves have not yet fully realised this. Political parties continue to cast about nervously, trying to sense the new polarization and failing to do so.

With the ruling structure and its component people as one very large group, the other can only consist of those who do not see themselves as primarily belonging to that structure. In its simplest terms, the polarization consists of sheep and goats. Both groups are completely trans-class. Sheep can consist of people from all social levels, from benefit-receivers to the Prime Minister. Goats likewise can be found from beggars to Royalty.

It must be stressed that the two groups represent clear-cut extremes, and that in reality most people settle somewhere in the middle, with leanings one way or the other, but the point to be made is that wealth and social class no longer represent (if they ever did) the essential polarity. Much more fundamentally, we lean either towards the uncreative or the creative - the depender on a structure or the free user of experience.

As I have already stressed, the structure has a basic need to protect and enhance itself, and so its component "sheep-people" are used by it to that end. "Goat-people", on the other hand, hardly realise that they exist as a group. Because their unifying factor is their sense of non-conformity, they are wary of bonding together lest this should destroy the very quality which makes them what they are. This is, of course, the central dilemma of the Green movement, which can be seen trying to organise without organising. A new, very delicate loose grouping is being evolved, based on voluntary ethical responsibility in the individual rather than any declared corporate policy, and this, although its members hardly realise it, constitutes the forward-looking half of the political divide today. In the future it will become much plainer, as squabbling over material gain by conflicting social groups is perceived to be an argument among sheep, with no fundamental ethical question being asked.

The question of whether work is purely a trading commodity or a rewarding activity in itself is the key one in determining to which group one belongs. It cuts across all activities, though some occupations have obvious leaning in one direction or the other. Nobody would sensibly become a teacher, for instance, exclusively for financial reward, and the saddest misfits within the profession are those who went into it because it seemed a safe job with an attainable promotion structure. Many, particularly in Primary schools, are goat-people, creative and empirical, constructing learning-potential out of the raw material of whatever surrounds them. Desperate efforts are being made to bring education into the sheep-system by reducing this creative freedom and making it more accountable, even to the extent of trying to apply "cost-effectiveness", which really is, as the old song says, like trying to carry rainbows home in a jar. Sheep, at their worst, can be extremely silly, but their combined forcefulness formalises absurdity into a stressful reality. They have immense impact.

Of the two groups, much the most effective at present is the structured one which is so firmly in power. Creative people, whether in science or the arts, in teaching or in business itself, recognise the intuitive, wayward quality in each other and laugh or groan over the increasing outrageousness of the prevailing system, but they fail to see themselves as capable of devising anything radically different. Awareness and humour and self-reliance illuminate contemporary writing and drama, particularly in Scotland, where a national dissent from the ruling system is endemic, and yet these qualities are not seen as the basis for a new and positive stance. They are confused with the traditional socialism which backed an oppressed class of industrial workers against "the bosses". With the collapse of that structure, the enemy is harder to identify, for it mingles in all walks of society in the form of the upwardly socially mobile and the insidious suggestion that all things have their price.

In the confusion, the thing which remains is the strong ethical basis of socialism. This has been forgotten (or pushed aside) in the horrors of Stalinism and in the economic failure of Eastern Europe, even though the failure has been largely brought about by the effects of a Cold War designed to do exactly what it has done. We have not appreciated that the underlying respect for the worth of the human soul which fired the Socialist movement is there still, waiting to find a new means of expression. It was not the idea which went wrong, but the methodology. In the effort to establish universal good-thinking, the system and the means of administering it became tighter and tighter, lending itself to control by narrow-minded and fanatical sheep-people. Rigidity can never be successfully opposed by rigidity, for such a conflict can only end in collapse of one side or another, and rigidity (never mind which) is left in control. The great strength of the present intangible and apparently ineffectual opposition to the system is its flexibility and the very insubstantiality which make it so hard to identify.

It is time, though, for creative people to come a little more closely together and realise that their outlook contains a positive strength. To do this will require clear-sightedness and courage on the part of people who already realise their own position, and an unstinting, rewardless generosity in helping others to find confidence in their own worth as human beings. We must look very carefully at the way creativity is regarded, and see the prejudice which lies behind the archetypical figures of the mad scientist, the absent-minded professor and the wild artist. There is a terrible self-limitation inherent in the anti-Bohemianism and anti-intellectualism of a political stance which automatically embraces the values of the disadvantaged against those of the advantaged, and it lives on in the so-called "anti-elite" attitude in education. Obviously, no child must be sacrificed in favour of another, but the very able must be given all they need to develop to an exceptional level, no matter in what direction. A re-stated belief in human potential must not be partial or conditional. The work of self-development is a universal need and is to the universal good. Only where such development is narrowed down to terms of self-indulgence does it become a threat, for it may then constitute an attack on others.

Determining the difference between development and indulgence is the immediate job of creativity, and that is why it is so vital to establish an enjoyable self-discipline within work. If discipline is imposed from outside, creativity is diverted into devising other, non-work forms of enjoyment. We must devote a lot of attention to understanding what creativity is and how it plays a vital part in our managing of ourselves in social and economic terms, for otherwise we will continue to accept the prevailing negative view. It is all too easy to go along with the conventional assumption that creativity is an unusual and specialised quality, present in only a few talented people. There is a self-gratification inherent in such a view which makes it attractive to the recognised artistic elite, and this is a strong factor in perpetuating it. To be able to think that one is special and inherently different from the common herd is a seductive notion, but it is ultimately destructive, for it leads to an inturned artistic arrogance which allows no breadth of vision. We must accept that creativity is an integral part of the passion of humankind which underlies all expression, whether political, religious or artistic.

If this proposition is accepted, then it will involve us in a sober and careful move towards political responsibility. People of a creative outlook have allowed themselves to be marginalised, partly because their horror at the philistinism of progress has made them feel unable to participate in it, but also because they have found it more comfortable to stand aside. There is a touch of complacency in accepting recognition as a person of exceptional talent, because all creative people know perfectly well that the success of their work is due to the extraordinary level of effort that is put into it rather than to any strange and unusual "inspiration". The effort represents a common ground between all people, and the factor which raises it to a high level is the belief that one's own existence is of extraordinary interest in itself.

With this in mind, the enhancing of self-confidence must obviously be of prime importance in encouraging a proper and responsible pride in one's own creativity and that of others. The psychologist's dictum that growing-up means doing things we do not want to do then seems doubly wrong. It betrays a quintessentially uncreative attitude, pushing the child towards the meek status of a sheep and sounding the death-knell of all self-confidence. A far more constructive suggestion would be that growing-up enables us to do what we want to do, and that the job of a child is to find out through extensive sampling of life exactly what its central desire really is.

When an apparently responsible adult tells a child (or, indeed, tells an adult) that his or her main duty must be the acceptance of unpleasant necessity, the effect is to destroy all faith in the future. If the depicted scenario is correct, then the reaction of a creative person can only be a determination to take evasive action. For a child with a strong sense of his or her own being, it confirms suspicions that the school is a hostile and crushing force which must be resisted, and for the adult, it reinforces depression. The intended effect is of course to bring about submission and an eventual adjustment within it, but such submission requires an abandoning of faith in one's own creative functioning. To a self-aware person, this is a state little better than death.

When this deathliness is associated with school-work, the effect is disastrous. The child is unable to perceive any benefit or enjoyment in the work provided, because it has been told that the purpose of the work is the very opposite. Therefore, enjoyment can only be found in activities directly related to the self and not to the school. The same thing is true of adults in their relationship to society. If their main duty is seen as the acceptance of unpleasantness, then society must seem to represent unpleasantness itself, and action against it is an expression of the desire for pleasure and an acknowledgement of the value of the self. In order to see such manifestations as graffiti and vandalism in their true light, we must understand this underlying motivation and its source. The virtues of endurance as a guiding principle can no longer be upheld, for in a commercialised society which offers virtually no creative expression through work, the frustration of personal expression constitutes a pressure which is beyond the strength of endurance to contain.

The frustration very commonly starts at school, though it is often heavily reinforced by parents who have themselves submitted to a state of uncomplaining endurance and so cannot understand the child's resentment. In a school where acceptance is held to be a prime virtue, teachers are tacitly encouraged to present their work in a way which confronts and challenges the children's instinct for life-enjoyment, in the belief that there is a valuable discipline in knuckling down to doing something unattractive. This is to set the discipline outwith the work itself, as a separate attribute, and so the work can be seen by the children as an instrument of the school's intended oppression. This suspicion is confirmed when discipline is enforced by personal attacks on the self-confidence such as, "What's so special about *you*?"

Equally damaging, though much more well-meaning, is the assumption that work is unpleasant because it is difficult, so it will be pleasanter if it is made easy. A teacher who holds this view has not taken on the creative attitude of presenting the work as a fascinating and highly complex thing in its own right, for he or she is still inwardly convinced that it is a pill which must be sugared. To this end, a plethora of work-sheets are produced which solicit the simplest of answers requiring only a tick placed in a box. The unspoken implication is clear to the child; "proper" work is too difficult and can only be given to more intelligent pupils. Low self-esteem settles in, together with a furious impatience on the part of the self-aware who are ravenous for a rich variety of experience and for constructive help in using it. Where there is a failure to present the work as a genuinely interesting occupation, there must be a counter-balancing drive in the children to find interest elsewhere, and thus the insistence on endurance breeds rebellion.

This is an easy enough fact to accept in principle, but to put an alternative attitude into practice required some fundamental thinking about the creative process. Children provide a rich source of information on the subject, because at an early age, they have not realised that there is anything except living itself, and experiencing it and expressing it. The followers of Zen would say that they are quite right. Be that as it may, there is a lot to be learned about the nature of the life process from those who are following it with single-minded devotion. Children irritate adults because of their complete unawareness of the conventions of behaviour which are designed to circumscribe the expression of feeling, but it is interesting to see that children are found much less irritating in less convention-bound countries, and particularly in countries where work is directly related to living. There is little that a tribal African child can do to annoy its mother, but the same behaviour in a city-dwelling British child can be found very stressful. The young child represents a constant human element in its natural state, a truth of existence against which we measure, not the child, but ourselves. No two children are alike, and they very quickly begin to reflect the influences which adults have on them, but the carrier-wave of feeling which sustains all human beings is less obscured in the child, if we can only perceive it.

Most people have at some time watched a small child draw a picture. A very young toddler will simply take a delight in the magical fact that the crayon leaves a mark behind it, and will scribble in the pleasure of hard and soft, fast and slow, being recorded on the paper. Later, representation begins, and the child is always completely certain of what the wavering lines mean, and will explain readily if asked. "It's Daddy." "It's a dog." But once, when pushed as to *how* she drew, a small girl said, "I think what I'm going to draw, and then I draw my think."

This is a precise statement of the creative process. Feeling-intelligence sorts out the phenomena which have been brought in by the senses, and comes up with an arrangement of them which reason judges to be satisfactory. The "think" has been made. It is then passed through activity to blossom as a specific creative act.

Because the activity stage of the process is the only one which the observer can witness, we assume that this constitutes creativity itself, so it seems irrational and mysterious. To come to terms with the whole function, we must recognise that the blossoming of expressive activity can only happen when the underlying "think" has been completed by the feeling- intelligence.

Children's art shows this with absolute clarity, because they do not draw with what adults consider to be photographic realism. They draw their "think" about the way things seems to be. All young children, on emerging from the scribble stage and the wavering-circle stage which is the first portrait, tackle the drawing of landscape. They do not draw the insides of houses, they draw the outside world with the sky shown as a narrow band along the top of the paper and the earth as a band along the bottom. In their experience, the sky is up and the ground is down, and like anyone else, they can only draw their experience. The fact that there is a white area in between these top and bottom strips does not enter into their calculations, and they regard questions about it as incomprehensible, much as we would if asked "What is behind the sky?" It is an irrelevant enquiry because it is not within out concept of what the sky is. With increasing age, children draw a deeper sky-band, and at last come to the recognition that it extends down to and in between any figures they have drawn, reaching all the way to the earth-band, to meet at the horizon.

The schemata of children's drawings have been well documented, and are remarkable for their accuracy. The speed at which children pass through the various stages of expression varies a lot, but they do all pass through them. As their awareness develops, more information is brought in and they are able to realise a more complete picture, but the process remains the same. Even in the case of the mature and meticulously naturalistic artist, it is the "think" which is painted and not the object itself. Poussin and Constable both paint landscape with the intention of rendering a realistic account of what they see, but they are two different men and each sees in his own way. Poussin cannot do anything but paint his own experience of being in a landscape, and the result is coloured by the way he felt about it, just as Constable's is. The tall trees and wide skies of the subject-matter provide only a common frame of reference against which the two men unwittingly depict themselves as witnesses.

In less "objective" painting, the frame of reference is partially or completely discarded and the artist knowingly paints what he or she feels. There is still a reference to things seen, for there is a conscious rearrangement of shapes and tones and elements from the observed world.

Because we do not recognise that the subject-matter of all expression is experience rather than the subject itself, we are perplexed by the contemporary art and music which does not trouble to relate itself closely to the experiences common to all of us. We search for something we can recognise as "real", but what we actually seek is familiarity - a repetition of an experience which has passed through our own awareness. If a composer should include a snatch of "Three Blind Mice" in a otherwise atonal composition, there would be a smile of recognition from the listeners because that sequence of notes exists already in the stored experience of any person brought up in the Western nursery-rhyme tradition. A re-experiencing of that sequence brings a comforting assurance that the self is in contact with a truth which other people recognise as well. It is a small soothing of insecurity. The same thing is true of joining in a well-known song or dancing to a tune with other people. It brings a very immediate sense of sharing.

For this reason, there is a deep mistrust of the unfamiliar. Children are urged to make their drawings "better", by which the adult usually means, "more recognisable" - in other words, closer to the experience which is stored in the adult's own mind. By the same token, the sound of children making up their own music offends many adults because they cannot listen in a relaxed and dispassionate way but seek for an echoing of the sounds they already carry in their own heads. Children's writing is often misunderstood because the appearance of it on the page, with its shakily-formed letters and unconventional spelling, is not familiar. I have on many occasions read the work of children aloud to adults, to be told afterwards, "I hadn't realised it said so much." The failure to communicate is not the child's, but the adult's.

A constructive approach to creativity must then begin with a recognition that nobody can express anything except their own experience and the way they feel about it. This lays the foundation of mutual respect and a solid understanding that we are all engaged in the same process. To push towards a product at all costs is often to short-circuit this process, and the increasingly popular "children as writers" schemes often fail to recognise this fact. A truly constructive lesson can consist of talking about the way an experience has seemed to be, with no words committed to paper at all. As children grow older, less and less time is given to talking about the experiencing of life; they are left to make what sense of it they can, and are offered no channel through which it may be explored and expressed. It is no wonder that teenagers suffer from an explosive build-up of unused feeling.

The use of feeling, however, requires skill, and it is here that adults commonly feel most uncertain. Having themselves received no training in expression, they find the whole area mysterious. This is why there is so often a retreat into the belief that creativity is the province of the talented alone, and that such people can safely be left to get on with it. At the worst, children are instructed to "write a poem", with no attempt being made to supply the imaginative experience on which to base such a task. "Freedom" of this kind puts a great strain on the child, who is being asked to give of him or herself with no fuel being offered. It is as if a hungry child is being asked to cook a meal for others rather than being given food.

The first step towards creative work must always be a review of what experiences are available as raw material. For a practising writer, this may take the form of an idea arising from the slightest of starting-points. A letter in a local paper complaining about the macabre implications of Hallowe'en could be the basis of a novel centred on religious bigotry, or a scrap of childhood memory could be re-formed to provide material for a children's book. Within every adult, there is a mass of such potential richness. Even if the stored experience is reviewed despairingly and rejected as repetitive and lacking in event, it may still be used. Kelman's "A Disaffection" contains nothing but the central character's sense of aridity, reflected in the trivial happenings which encompass a man trapped in his own lack of self-knowledge, and yet it is a powerful book. Remembering the image of the blastocyst, a unity of the incoming phenomenon fertilised by the emotion which it engenders, we can see that the raw material for any form of expression consists of experience coupled with our own reaction to it. We can rearrange it in any way we like, discarding the conventions of time and space if we want to work in the fields of the supernatural or in fantasy, but above all, we have to work at it. The only problem is, *how* to work at it. If creativity begins in the state where the proposed artefact does not exist and ends with a finished product, how does one identify what form the work should take?

The simplest answer is to think of the creative process as very much like the selection undertaken by the adept shopper. One starts with infinite possibilities, and each choice makes the field a little narrower. Eventually, all alternatives have been discarded in favour of the one selected. In my own case, my mother enforced a creative attitude from an early age. "You can have a cake", she said as we stood in front of the baker's window. "Choose which one you want." The array of meringues and macaroons and iced fancies was bewildering, and I was suddenly aware that choosing a single one meant un-choosing all the others. Whichever one I chose, I was going to regret it. "You choose", I begged, unwilling to take the responsibility - but she was adamant. "If you don't choose, you shan't have one at all." Faced with such an ultimatum, I chose. It would have been much easier not to, just as it is always easier to accept or grumble about someone else's decisions than it is to make one's own.

Choosing is the most essential element of the creative process, and so the child (or adult) as chooser needs to sort out the criteria by which choosing is done. First, there is the question of what kind of end-product is wanted. If, for instance, some kind of writing is to be undertaken, what sort is it to be? A poem, a story, a report? Funny, serious, sad? Factual, historic, romantic, fantastic? The answers can only be found by inspecting the material which lies within the feeling-intelligence and sensing the appropriate vehicle for it. Maybe the potential idea centres round the visit of a country lad to a big city - will it be told in the first person or observed by a dispassionate narrator. Will it be serious or funny? Slowly, the generalities are assessed. The potential nature of the piece is still very wide. Will the hero be witless or cunning, dogged by bad luck or possessed of charm which rescues him from sticky situations? *What* sticky situations? In such a way, the self-questioning moves from the general to the particular. From the boundless possibilities of plot, a specific course of action must be chosen, but this must be convincing, so it must fit with the planned personalities of the people involved and the place where it is all happening. What does it look like, what do people say, and in what words? *Why* do they say these words to each other and what will be the effect?

Much of this questioning happens before anything is written down at all, just as a painter will conceive what kind of picture he or she is going to paint before the canvas is set on the easel. An athlete who is about to execute a vault will stand for a long moment in preparation, trying to be absolutely clear about the sequence of movement he or she is going to perform. Just as the child "drew her think", so the athlete or dancer or even darts player moves to delineate a "think" and the writer writes it and the speaker speaks it.

In every case, the choosing of material for the "think" is the fundamental process.

The majority of educational procedures do not require any exercise of the choosing-process, and the discipline exerted by the teacher has the purpose of ensuring that unwanted alternatives do not creep in. It is thus a compressing, limiting force rather than an expanding one. In a creative approach, questioning is integral to the work, and the necessary discipline must ensure that the questions are related to the onward progress of what is being attempted. Lengthy "red herrings" involving a mass of detail about some minor character, for instance, may need to be kept under control and, as the work develops, there must be a constant and very sensitive scrutiny of what has been written in case it is not serving the intended whole product as fittingly as it should. At the last stage, every nuance of expression and timing (as controlled by punctuation and sentence-construction) must be carefully questioned. The writer must work as his or her own reader, asking all the time whether the reader's experience of what is written is what the writer really meant.

Discipline in these circumstances becomes an internal affair of the utmost scrupulousness, and it takes many years to achieve it. Some of those years may, if a child is lucky, be spent within full-time education, but for many, this kind of work and self-discovery does not begin until after leaving school and, often, after time spent in recovering from the conviction that anything to do with books must be boring.

Nobody can expect to have much control over external events. We all hope to avoid unpleasant and painful experiences, but there is no way in which we can guarantee to do so. The road accident or illness, the disastrous relationship or intolerable job or loss of someone beloved exists as a potential which surrounds us throughout our lives, and no amount of careful curtailing of risky activity can give us immunity from these happenings. In other words, we are not in control of the incoming experience which forms half of our creative fuel. The other half, consisting of our own reaction to it and use of it, is, on the other hand, very much within our control, but only if we recognise the difference between our immediate emotional response and our subsequent refinement of that response into expression.

The kind of person we recognise as "imbalanced" has very little feeling-intelligence between emotion and reason, so there is a reduced ability to go through the leisured self-questioning which balances all possibilities. Instead, a strong emotional impulse will be forced quickly through into reason, there to be given some kind of rationale which may be quite nonsensical when related to larger perspectives. Thus a man annoyed in some way by his wife may declare furiously,"You women are all the same!" and then proceed to detail the short-comings of the sex which his immediate emotional prompting dictates. The same, of course, may be true of the reverse situation. Somebody with a well-developed feeling-intelligence can, in the same circumstances, review his or her own reactions to the situation and give a better-considered opinion of how things seem to be, offering a constructive opening-up of views in which the partner may participate.

For these reasons of self-understanding as well as for the more specific ones of satisfaction in expression, it is becoming urgently important that creativity, with its emphasis on the development of feeling-intelligence, should be brought more actively into education. The rewards in terms of emotional control and peace of mind are incalculable, but this has not been understood by many of our most powerful figures. On June 28th, 1990, Peter Morgan, as director general of the Institute of Directors, said that it was time to discard the idea that education was "to humanise our inner nature" rather than to help people to earn a living. He called for work-experience to begin as early as seven years old. His motives seem questionable.

Work-experience, like all experience, is valuable, but only when the experiencer is valued rather than the work. In many fields, active experience is the only way to learn. To speak a language, one must speak; learning from a book may produce the ability to read and write a language, but not to speak it. A dancer can only learn a choreographic routine by doing it, and a potter cannot throw a pot without handling the clay and learning how it relates to his or her own muscle-control and inner "think" of how the evolving pot should be. These things are very different from the assumption which Peter Morgan expressed - that work needs people and that it will give them all the reward they need as long as they carry it out according to its demands.

To encourage creativity can be no more than a superficial dressing-up of the curriculum unless it nurtures the asking of questions and helps to establish a framework within which these questions can lead to the best choice of eventual expression. In such a co-operative system order is kept by a consensus of agreement rather than by enforcement, and all people, whether children or adults and whether socially important in conventional terms or not, are valued equally for the fact that they are alive and aware. Ready-made ideas of how things should be done are useful, for creative thinking is very tiring and it is sometimes a relief to be given a rest from it, but ultimately, every person must devise his or her own way of making sense out of the confusing business of being alive.

This poem was written by a sixteen-year-old girl. Her workmanlike attention to the nature of her own feelings is impeccable.

Sunday Morning

I am not in the mood to go to church today.
Starched and strained sopranos are an ache away
From thrilling larks and churring wrens.
The people there are uninspired, their minds
So full of dust, no room for dew
Or fire; but my virtue
Is to stand in the forest by the chortling burn
And the chaffinch that derides me from its lofty
Pine-pulpit; so, to gain humility, I turn around, I am baptised
In the year-long Eastertide.
I see a tree and lean my face against its
Green split jigsaw bark, look up
At its corolla of spiking
Spokes, look down and
Shock
Dark bloodshock
Body of doe bullet-ripped, her eyes
Still open, body buzzing with flies.

I run to the stream in confusion, I want
To be cleansed, but my font
Has been tainted, it stinks of green polluted scum,
In its purity's place I have delirium.
If this decay is my religion's truth
I'll go to church. Tripping over brambles, bricks,
Barbed wire, I lurch into my pew.
A baby is christened and cries,
Sweat steams, and my cheeks flush.
It's hard to believe in God when I can't hush
The voice that rages and screams at all his lies.

Lynn Dunlop

112

The future is too interesting and dangerous to be entrusted to any predictable, reliable agency. We need all the fallibility we can get. Most of all, we need to preserve the absolute unpredictability and total improbability of our connected minds. That way, we can keep open all the options, as we have in the past.

Lewis Thomas

Practice and Theory

The conventionally-accepted idea that theory must precede practice is a narrow and essentially uncreative one. It pre-supposes that the person who devises the theory has encompassed such a complete range of possibility that nothing unexpected can happen. If it does happen, then there are frantic efforts to cover the embarrassing event with a cloak of previously-conceived explanation, rather as a naked person appearing in public must instantly be wrapped in a blanket.

To be lastingly tenable, a theory has to embrace every conceivable aspect of the unknown. It can only do this by relating its proposition to the fact that our knowledge is bounded by mystery. We do not know what living is or what time is, or how to imagine what there was before the beginning of everything or, conversely, the nature of a state of existence which has lasted and will last for ever, world without end, amen. In thinking of such things, the mind returns, dazed, to its own small but central existence, for it cannot know how things are. It can only sense them as best it can.

Co-ordinate geometry builds up a picture of any given phenomenon by the process of combining several viewpoints. The resulting conclusion appears to be a close representation of what seems to be true, but if a totally new factor should be established - about, for instance, the nature of time - the whole structure might be seen afresh. While the attitude is open, that freshness can be preserved and new perceptions can be incorporated without difficulty, but to let this happen, we must cherish the value of uncertainty. The creative view accepts absolutely that there is no fixed certainty. We are in an ongoing state of evaluation, and can report nothing but the impressions received by our own minds.

The co-ordinate principle is surprisingly well-established. A single person expressing anger and distress at the sight of a starving child will have little effect, but when the same experience produces the same reaction from a large number of other people, the thing which they all react to begins to acquire a more readily believed-in truth. It is a factor which has been formalised in law-making. A dozen witnesses who concur about what they have seen will carry far more weight than a single one.

Underlying this trustworthiness is sheer practicality. Witness is of more value than opinion. In view of this, it is strange that so many aspects of modern life are dominated, in effect, by opinion. A theory is one or more person's opinion of the way things work or can be made to work, and the theories tend currently to regard themselves as possessed of certainty. Our rejoicing at the collapse of economic systems different from our own implies that we are quite certain that our own is good. In practice, many people will bear witness from personal experience that it is not good. The co-ordinates from whose combined viewpoints the truth is pictured have not been openly chosen, as they would have been if uncertainty had been admitted; they have been selectively chosen, so as to produce the picture which the current theory has settled on as the right one.

The effect of this trust in theory is very immediate. It affects the jobs we do and the buildings we live in as well as the way in which we are expected to think. "The planning stage" is accepted as a necessary fore-runner of any large-scale action, and the planning is based on the latest theories as to how things should be done. The theories, in turn, are based (or so we are told) on a consensus of informed opinion and on the results of the latest research. There is a feeling among the general public that something is wrong with the opinions and research, for the decisions they lead to often have very little bearing on the reality of ordinary people's experience. New buildings, for instance, frequently fail to be pleasant or comfortable despite ever more rigid regulations about ceiling heights and window areas. Factors other than experiential ones bring a heavy influence to bear on the problem of construction, so the building which is eventually put up is the solution to problems which are not founded in real human experience, but have been created by economic limitation coupled with an uneasy compromise between the personal architectural tastes of the planning committee.

This is a typical result of putting theory before practice. Old cottages, conversely, were built with virtually no theory involved at all, usually by the people who intended to live in them. They were deficient in such things as damps courses and their ceilings were too low and their windows too small and nothing was quite straight, and yet we take photographs of them to put on chocolate boxes and to chop up for reassembly as jigsaws. Having started as valueless, old cottages now command a high price because of their "character". They provide a living environment which feels natural and comfortable and which has an inherent beauty. They are the product of practicality.

The same principle can still be applied. With no sacrifice of building standards, there can be a marked shift towards the practical simply by researching the opinion of those who will actually live in the building rather than the opinion of theorists. Where this happens, as it has done, for example, in a Housing Trust refurbishment of old tenement blocks in London, the tenants contribute their own living experience to the proposals and the architect (a woman, in this case) can add this to her own imagination and technical knowledge. The result is that a previously seedy area of Grays Inn Road is now a pleasant environment in which the tenants take a shared pride. Practice has preceded theory, and so the problem solved is the real problem, and not one which has been designed by the architect along with the building. A joint creativity has been put to work.

In the larger areas of economic organisation, there is virtually no opportunity at all for consultation with potentially constructive public opinion. The creative selectivity of ordinary people is valued for only one thing - in the choice of how to spend money. As Margaret Thatcher so notoriously said, "There is no such thing as society." Instead, there are customers. In this area, the man in the street (and woman, and child) suddenly becomes important. Shopping is a choice-making activity to be encouraged, for without it, cash will not flow from buyer to seller and the economic machinery will run out of fuel. Shops are given priority treatment, with multi-storey car parks close by for maximum convenience. They are protected from the weather by translucent roofing and supplied with escalators, fountains, pink neon lights and soothing music. It is a lovingly-constructed environment at the far extreme from the dirt and ugliness of the housing schemes where people of low spending power are put to conduct their economically insignificant lives.

Shopping is now the most popular leisure-time activity in Britain. The reason for this runs deeper than the intensive wooing of the customer. It turns on the fact that shopping now represents, for most people, the only remaining area in which they are encouraged to express a creative choice. It is, as shopkeepers well know, an ongoing need. The main aim of a shop is not to provide a satisfactory purchase which will send the customer away with no further need to return, but to titillate the appetite for spending. For every item bought, a thousand others remain unbought and beckoning. The pleasure is not, for many people, the return home with a new article but the experience of shopping itself.

In choosing and evaluating, the creative function is brought into active use, even though the use is ultimately an empty one. It provides an opportunity for the asking of the basic creative questions; do I like this? Does it suit its purpose? Does it fit with what I already have? Does it say about me what I want it to say? These are the same questions a writer asks of draft work done the previous day. To the question-asker, they seem very interesting and central. They are not being asked at someone else's behest or as part of a set task - they are invented by the self and for the self. Shopping is a tiring occupation, not merely because it involves trudging about in over-heated and airless environments, but because of the exercising of choice. Shopping is work, but because it is creative work which can be enjoyed, it is thought of as play. Again, we come back to the confusion of work with earning. Play can in fact be very hard work. A tennis player at the end of a hard match will be exhausted. The exhaustion has nothing to do with the fact that a professional player may earn money at his or her chosen sport. It is the playing which is hard work, not the earning. Similarly, shopping as a leisure or "play" activity is in fact creative

116

work. The newness of the purchased article wears off in a day or two, leaving a desire to go shopping again and in time the desire becomes the only permanent thing, settling in as a vague conviction that happiness can be bought eventually, if one has enough money and keeps on shopping. It is, of course, an illusory conviction, but it serves to keep the majority of people firmly within the grip of the economic system, just as an addict to any other illusion must remain within the grip of the system which supplies it. We are the junkies of capitalism.

In all areas where the individual person cannot claim the status of a customer, it is made very plain that his or her creative choosing is not an element in the transaction. Public transport, for instance, gives only minimal regard to the way in which the individual traveller experiences the service which is provided. Significantly, travellers are now referred to as "customers", as if to reassure them on this very point, and yet the main aim remains to move them about as cheaply as possible while extorting, as a letter from British Rail to myself once put it, "the maximum fare which the market will stand." Those who will consider paying extra to travel "executive" class are wooed with free drinks and extra legroom, but they are the only people who are offered travel in the spirit of a shop offering attractive goods. For the rest, if an undersized "Sprinter" is cheaper to run than a proper train, it will be run, regardless of the resulting overcrowding and discomfort. To travel is less important than to pay.

The fundamental reason why our latent creativity has become so remote from the essential business of life is that it has no relationship to our economic structure except where it is linked to it through buying or selling. The making of money is assumed to be the basic purpose of life, and it is further assumed to be a good purpose. The current economic theory is that wealth will trickle down through the layers of society from those at the top who hold most money to those at the bottom who have least, and there is an implicit suggestion that the same process also dispenses virtue. If money-making is good, it is argued, then those who succeed at it must be the best and those who fail at it are the worst. It is a neat theory, for it contains its own impetus. Since poverty is associated with unworthiness, failure to make money can very easily be seen also as a failure in ethical terms, doubling the punishment. Seeing the resulting distress, others feel doubly impelled to try and function successfully within the economic system.

To the great mass of ordinary people, it seems unfair and inexplicable that there should be this association between wealth and virtue, together with its condemnatory converse. In the normal experience of life, it is manifestly untrue that poor people are less good than rich ones, or that they can be held responsible for failing to acquire a higher degree of privilege - and yet the assumption is there. It is not new. The common reminiscence of the elderly - "We didn't have much money when I was a child, but we were happy" - has a touch of special pleading about it, as does the old dirge, "She was poor but she was honest...." If there is any doubt about the underlying implication, one has only to consider the converse. "We had a lot of money when I was a child, but we were happy." "She was rich but she was honest...." These observations are the stuff of satire, for they are ironic and politically charged, running counter to the status quo.

The assumption that wealth and virtue are indissociable has grown up like a vigorous weed to prevent the flourishing of creativity. It was not an accidental seeding, but something more akin to the run-away success of the rabbit in Australia or the rhododendron in the Scottish Highlands, usurping all available resources. Sir James Frazer, in his 1922 study of magic and religion, "The Golden Bough", is unabashed in his support for the imposition of the idea. "As soon as the tribe ceases to be swayed by the timid and divided counsels of the elders, and yields to the direction of a single strong resolute mind, it becomes formidable to its neighbours and enters on a career of aggrandisement....For extending its sway, partly by force of arms, partly by the voluntary submission of weaker tribes, the community soon acquires wealth and slaves." Without a trace of embarrassment, he advocates the destruction of cultures which exist in a loosely-grouped stasis of contained creativity, substituting the notion of economic progress at the expense of other groups.

Very clearly, such an initiative takes as its most fundamental principle an assumption that the feelings of the tribe are worthless. The fact that the group has managed to go on living non-agressively for hundreds, perhaps even thousands of years, is not seen as admirable but as disgraceful. Subtlety of feeling and democratic expression of opinion are dismissed as timidity and division. "At this early epoch", Frazer asserts, "despotism is the best friend of humanity and, paradoxical as it may sound, of liberty." The freedom to oppress others is heady stuff.

Frazer's view of life remains virtually unchallenged. "Development " is the battle-cry and the feelings of the people concerned are ignored. There is a scream of protest from hundreds of people every time a new area of natural ground is desecrated in the name of road-building or defence against a mythical enemy or storage of poisonous materials, and this scream is an expression of real pain, deeply felt by the men and women who experience it, but the tribe is not thought to know what is best for it, and despotism is forced on us as our best friend.

The effective expression of feeling has in this century been contained within what is known as "art". It has been channelled away from what used to be a process inherent in the conduct of life itself, and prevented from having any influence on those who control the so-called "development" of our society. As Frazer makes clear, it is a pre-requirement of such development that it shall free itself from the influence of popular feeling - except, of course, where such feeling has a direct bearing on profitability. The Campaign for Real Ale, for instance was a huge success because it constituted a clear intention of purchasers to divert their money towards a preferred commodity. The peace movement, although representative of a far wider and larger section of public opinion, cannot express itself through purchasing and so it cannot exert any economic leverage on official thinking. Since no other kind of leverage is recognised, such opinion is easy to ignore. The gulf between human feeling and administrative policy is very wide.

It may be objected that creativity has no need to direct itself into political or sociological activity, and this is perfectly true. The argument is cast in wider terms than that. To think that creativity should be encouraged only because it empowers people to have a direct effect on their circumstances is to run the risk of harnessing creative thinking to a specific purpose, with the "approved line" and the censorship which will inevitably result. The point is that a new awareness of the basic nature of creativity can alter the way in which people envisage themselves and their relationship to their surroundings. It does not matter whether writing has a direct political content or not; to be a creative person is not to be a propagandist but a fully-aware human being. A society composed of fully-aware people will not be an inert and easily-dominated one.

In recent centuries, such awareness has been the enemy of what Frazer terms progress, therefore it is a quality which has been systematically reduced. The British "stiff upper lip" is not the sign of brave endurance which its admirers have always assumed; it is in fact a determination to show no feeling. Very few women, to their credit, ever acquire this characteristic: it is found most commonly in men who belong to the ruling classes, as one would expect. The expressionless face is a demonstration that its owner has a proper disregard for feeling and is therefore a suitable person to be put in charge of others.

The lack of connection between feeling and administration has obvious tangible results. Take, for instance, the question of poverty. For the person who suffers it, poverty is a continual state of anxiety and deprivation. It means being cold when the weather is cold and queueing outside the hall where a jumble sale is being held so as to get first go at rummaging for cheap garments. It means that children's feet are constricted in over-tight shoes because new ones are expensive, and that adults' feet are wet when it rains. This is an ongoing reality which the awareness cannot avoid. It is the *feeling* of poverty, the practice, so to speak, as opposed to the theory. The theory of poverty exists as a different reality, couched in statistics. The number of people living below the official poverty-line or without housing can be detailed objectively, with no feeling involved. It can be (and usually is) computed by a machine, very satisfactorily.

Of the two truths, the objective one is the easier to consider as a basis for action. Statistics can be passed round a committee, but it is extremely unlikely that a cardboard-box-dweller will be invited in to join the proceedings. The statistics should, as chairpersons are wont to remark, "speak for themselves". That is to say, they should evoke in those who peruse them an understanding of what they really mean. It should be possible to interpret them so perceptively as to share in the human feeling which they represent. Occasionally a committee member will exclaim that the figures are appalling or give some other expression to a feeling reaction. There will be polite agreement, but the usual response in such a gathering is to shuffle papers and cough in faint embarrassment while someone rephrases the comment in more acceptably dispassionate language.

If more people had confidence that feeling can and must be a valued part of human activity, then it should be possible to bring the two aspects of truth more closely together, so that they co-exist as a single totality. The pattern of this single but double-aspected truth is present in the nature of life at its most fundamental level. Wave-function and particle-function seem contradictory, but they express the dual nature of every particle. Equally, in macrocosmic terms, according to the model suggested earlier in this book , the centre of the wheel of time represents one essence and the centre of the self another, but their intimate connectedness is the unity of life itself.

We have sought to divide this unity with increasing vigour throughout recent years. Our splitting of the atom is perhaps symbolic, an opening of Pandora's box which has let loose an evil which cannot be contained. There are many aspects of it, but prime among them is the splitting of reason from feeling. Creativity, as we have seen, takes both these qualities, bringing them into a wholeness of constructive use.

The problem is a practical one. The feeling of need for creativity is widespread, but we lack guidance or an example to turn to. Our search for an authoritative guru is misplaced, for external authority of any kind, no matter how benign, continues our sense of being dependent on an outside agency. We should, instead, look to children.

This is not to propose any sentimental imitation of childishness. It is not the performing abilities of children which are valuable, for these are learned from adults: it is the underlying mental freedom. A child can combine acute awareness of the "real" surroundings with the imaginative agility which enables him or her to be inside the being of another person or animal, whether real or fictional. At about eight years old, there is a period of intense living, before theory starts to impose its dead hand. As Kenneth Grahame writes of adults in his marvellous book of childhood reminiscences, The Golden Age, "We ...could have told them what real life was. We had just left it outside, and we were all on fire to get back to it."

To identify creativity as an intrinsic process of living must involve a recognition of the fact that the human spirit is present and complete in us from birth. We learn nothing but techniques. If the spirit is recognised and respected, then the learning of these techniques can be tackled with energy. The present "child-centred" movement in teacher training has still got it wrong, because the insistence that learning must be fun flinches away from a solid recognition of the fact that the child is of immense worth, and deserves to be helped to work hard.

Occasionally a young person manages to be heard. Magnus Brooke, a pupil from West Yorkshire, had this to say in The Guardian in 1990. "It seems ironical that a school whose primary function is to cultivate the human intellect denies the very power it should encourage by excluding the pupil voice on matters of fundamental educational concern." He points out that "the lack of participation in the education system carries over into the life of work. Dictation in industry, just as in schools, alienates and divides, producing hostility to authority, even violence." He speaks with the sophistication of an adult, but has retained the pragmatic common-sense of childhood.

Superficially, common-sense would seem to be far removed from the qualities of imagination and identification with other things, and yet they all answer the same question - "Why not?" Imagining is practical. A sofa can very simply be thought of as a boat, or one's arms (especially the elbows) the piston rods of a locomotive.

If one is quite used to being Robin Hood or Black Beauty at will, it is easy to think up all kinds of possibilities in adult life and to use whatever comes to hand in order to make them real. The capacity for creative improvisation is, in effect, a remnant of the survival instinct, and it is always valued in times of abnormal pressure. All soldiers know that it is the sergeant rather than the officer who will solve immediate problems of making life tolerable in embattled conditions.

In practical terms, imagination is immensely useful. When living on very little money, an imaginative person can make creative use of cheap basic food and devise amusements for children which cost nothing, whereas someone thoroughly conditioned as an unthinking consumer will go on buying frozen food and plastic toys. The difference in approach is superficially thought to be a class one, turning on the self-confidence of a bourgeois background, but this is almost deliberately self-deceptive, reinforcing the myth that people are only poor through their own fault. There is a great wealth of creativity among people of no inherited middle-class confidence whatever. Women in particular use constant ingenuity to make a supportive and interesting environment for their children, even in the most unpromising of circumstances.

It seems likely that this creative practicality will become even more valuable in the future. Every sign points to a growing disillusion with the systems which currently control us. All over the world, small countries struggle to be released from the authority of large ones, and small groups within countries defend or reclaim their own language and customs. We begin to sense that an era is ending, and that no trust can be felt in the present holders of power. A commonly-voiced opinion is that "They're all the same." This is not apathy but disillusion, which is a very different thing. Apathy is uncaring but disillusion sees no way in which caring can matter.

121

The only way in which our caring can be constructively expressed is between ourselves, in the small local groups of people who know each other. The pattern of double-aspect totality is present in government just as it is in the basic building-blocks of life. At one extreme, there must be a corporate world authority to act as a control over national madness, but its counterpart is the self-government of small groups, connected to each other by consenting co-operation. This is where creative imagination will be vital, for a fundamental reshaping of our administrative systems must lie ahead of us if the human race is to continue.

As people all over the world have accurately sensed, the impending global crisis will eventually force us to abandon the deluded notion that we can go on endlessly expanding our activities. This is why the political squabble over power and possessions no longer fundamentally interests us. It seems futile and irrelevant in the face of the nemesis which threatens us. The Green movement has not yet succeeded in establishing (or even perhaps in understanding) that it represents an attempt to look ahead to the new, planet-related social and economic system which we must evolve, but thousands of people know it instinctively, and can only express it in a disgust and impatience with the irrelevant political maneuverings which continue to be presented as important news.

The means of change have yet to be devised, but it seems certain that the imaginative perceptivity of ordinary people will become a vitally necessary factor. If a co-operative network of groups is ever to put into practice the true principles of democracy, then the quality of each person in each group becomes very important.

A fragile web of trust and confidence already exists between people, particularly among women, who are prepared to care for each other in a practical way, without the exchange of money. This web, I suggest, constitutes a necessarily insubstantial blueprint for the future. It has flexibility and strength, but these qualities can only develop through the development of individuals in discovering their own latent creativity and, through this, learning again to respect the human spirit.

Masel the American loose in Scotland — what chance would you give him?

Self-styled failed folk-performer and holder of a stupid PhD, Elliot Masel flees San Francisco and a broken marriage to take part in Glasgow's Culture Month. His scholarly impersonations of Sixties musical icons are hijacked by the wily and delectable Katy and the constantly inebriated Professor Longman, and turned into the most amazing stage show ever seen in Culture City. Masel's quest for love and accomplishment looks set for fulfillment, but the ghosts of his past draw him deeply into his own psyche.

In Masel Mark Smith offers us a tragi-comic Everyman for our time.

**"See Glasgow, see Culture . . .
Life is a cold bowl of chicken soup —
and then you die."**

a collection of some of the best short fiction
from early editions of West Coast Magazine.

edited by

Kenny MacKenzie & Joe Murray

includes stories from:

John Cunningham, Janice Galloway,
Wilma Murray, Agnes Owens and many more

Available from all leading Bookshops

£4.99 ISBN 1-873899-00-9

The Mating Of Dinosaurs

By

William Oliphant

This is the first full collection of poetry from one of Glasgow's most popular writers. Drawing on the best of limited edition booklets such as The Impact of Television on the Plumhead Parakeet, The Seamstress In The Nudist Camp and Devil's Dozen, as well as the many anthologies and magazines Oliphant has contributed to in the past, this volume is long overdue.

Born in 1920, William Oliphant left school at fourteen and worked in a variety of jobs servicing radio, television and electronic keyboard instruments. In the early fifties he was a member of Edward Scoullar's writers' group *The Wolves of Buchanan Street*. He had some success writing short fiction but gave up writing for a number of years to concentrate on bringing up his family. He began writing poetry in 1983.

The Mating Of Dinosaurs £5.95 ISBN 0-873899-30-0

The Gringo Trees

by J. William Doswell

Life in the Village of San Sebastian in El
Salvador is poor, but not as bad as it could
be. A living can be eked out from the seas
and shoreline of the Pacific. Until, that is, the
army is posted there to prevent campesinos
from smuggling arms, with a devastating
effect on the lives of the villagers.

J. William Doswell is an American who lives
in Virginia in the southern part of the United
States. He has been a marine, a journalist, a
political lobbyist and a member of the Central
Intelligence Agency. Married with three
grown sons, he now writes fiction full time

The Gringo Trees £4.99

ISBN 1-873899-05-X

West Coast Magazine

West Coast Magazine has, over the last four years, established itself as one of the most important outlets for new writing in Scotland. Brian Whittingham, Bill Oliphant, J. William Doswell, Janice Galloway and John Cunningham, are among those who have counted appearing in the magazine as an early landmark in their writing career.

West Coast Magazine ISSN 0963 - 732X

4 issues

UK   £ 8.00
Overseas £16.00

Write to:

West Coast Magazine
Dolphin Arts Centre
7 James Street
Bridgeton
Glasgow G40 1BZ